Zwemmer

£37-80
13-10-94

11082✓

"**Art, like morality,** consists of drawing the line somewhere." G.K. CHESTERTON

American Illustration 12

The 12th annual of American
editorial, book, advertising, posters/maps,
graphics, unpublished work and video.

Edited by Edward Booth-Clibborn
Designed by Frankfurt Balkind Partners

editor)
Edward Booth-Clibborn

publisher)
Kenneth Fadner

designers)
Kent Hunter and Ruth Diener,
Frankfurt Balkind Partners

cover and divider illustrations)
Johan Vipper,
Frankfurt Balkind Partners

production manager)
Tina Moskin,
Frankfurt Balkind Partners

production coordinators)
Mark Heflin and Jay Heflin

printed by)
Dai Nippon, Hong Kong

special thanks to)
Parsons School of Design for providing
the space and equipment for the
American Illustration 12 competition.

**The artwork and the caption infor-
mation** in this book have been sup-
plied by the entrants. While every effort
has been made to ensure accuracy,
American Illustration does not under any
circumstances accept any responsibility
for errors or omissions.

If you are a practicing illustrator, artist,
or student, and would like to **submit
work** to the next annual competition,
write to)
American Illustration
5 East 16th Street, 11th floor
New York, NY 10003
212.647.0874

distributor to the USA Trade)
Rizzoli International Publications
300 Park Avenue South
New York, NY 10010-3599

**distributor to United Kingdom
and World Direct Mail)**
Internos Books
12 Percy Street
London W1P 9FB U.K.

book trade for the rest of the world)
Hearst Books International
1350 Avenue of the Americas
New York, NY 10019

Contents

Introduction

Edward Booth-Clibborn of **American Illustration** and this year's jury:

Gail Anderson, Richard **Baker**, Jessica Helfand, **Kent Hunter**, Mirko Ilić, **Mark** Koudys, Kandy Littrell.

6

Editorial

Illustrations for **newspapers and** their suppliments,

and consumer, trade, **and technical magazines** and periodicals.

14

Books

Cover and **interior illustrations for all types of** fiction and non-fiction books.

112

Advertising

Illustrations **used for advertising in consumer, trade** and professional magazines.

144

Posters / Maps

Poster illustrations used for **consumer products, institutions and spec**ial events /

Maps for ma**gazines and prom**otional use.

154

Graphics

Illustrations for bro**chures, record albu**ms, self-promotion.

160

Unpublished Work

Comissioned **but unpublished** illustrations,

and personal work pr**oduced by professi**onals and students.

174

Video

Video for television comm**ercials, corporate** and self-promotion.

200

Index

Names and **addresses of contributing artists; na**mes of art directors, designers,

publications, publishers, design **groups, advertising** agencies, writers and clients

who were involved in **the creation and** use of these images.

204

Introduction

portrait by Adrian George

The judging for this edition of "American Illustration" took place in March of 1993 with a jury of seven people, all of whom I would like to thank for their time, enthusiasm, wit and wisdom. ✗ **With** the publication of this twelfth annual we have reached a point where a definite style of American illustration has emerged. This is especially true of the work from the younger people whose submissions we have accepted over the last few years; people who have since become very successful as American illustrators. ✗ **But** there is a disturbing trend behind this success. ✗ **Put** simply, too many people are copying other people's work. ✗ **Th**is year, for example, the jury rejected quite a number of items produced by people who, to put it bluntly, can only be described as rip-off artists. ✗ **Tr**agically, the artists who suffer most are the people like Edward Sorel, Guy Billout, Bob Blechman and Brad Holland whose highly original work is so often plagiarized. ✗ **Who** is to blame for this? ✗ **I** fear that it begins in art schools, where students are pressured into producing portfolios designed to get them work, rather than to show off the individual talents. ✗ **It** is also a sad reflection of the visual communications business in general, where people are increasingly prepared to pay less for a copyist than they would for the original thinker. ✗ **It** seems to me that there is only one way to stamp this out, and that is that copyists' work should not be recognized. ✗ **Our** jury has done their part, particularly by dismissing every copyist's submission and including the exceptionally imaginative work for the windows of Bloomingdales by Jessie Hartland and Josh Gosfield's fine work for Barneys' windows. I believe it takes real talent to be able to see the broad applications open to illustration and then have the vision to carry fresh ideas through to the end. ✗ **It** is work like this – and much else beside – which shows that, after twelve years, "American Illustration" is very much here to stay as the benchmark of excellence in a highly competitive world.

Edward **B**ooth-**Cl**ibborn

Jes**sica Helf**and

Jessica Helfand has been design director at the "Philadelphia Inquirer Sunday Magazine" since July, 1990. During this time, the magazine has won over 60 awards in graphic design and photography from the Society of Newspaper **Designers and the American Institute of Graphic Arts, among others. ∞ Prior to this, she was a designer with Roger Black Studio in New York, where she worked on the redesigns of numerous American and European publications including "Mother Earth News," "McCalls" and "Grazia." ∞ She has lectured at the University of Pennsylvania, and has been guest critic at Yale University, Temple University's School of Journalism, University of the Arts and Tyler School of Art in Philadelphia. Helfand judged this year's Illustrator's Club of Washington show, and last year's competition sponsored by the Philadelphia chapter of the American Society of Magazine Photographers. Her work** has appeared in numerous publications including the Print Regional Design Annual and the Communication Arts annuals in both photography and illustration. She holds a B.A. and a M.F.A. in graphic design from Yale University.

favorite deadly sin: lust

portrait by **Gregory Manchess**

Kandy Littrell

Kandy Littrell is senior art director for covers at "Newsweek." In addition to her past freelance work with Random House and Houghton Mifflin, she has held various posts at "The New York Times Magazine," "New England Monthly," and "Rolling Stone." ∞ As an illustrator, Kandy's work has appeared in such publications as "Ms. Magazine," "National Lampoon," "Psychology Today," and "Savvy." Throughout her career, her efforts have been awarded by The Art Directors Club of New York, Communication Arts, and SPD, to name a few.

favorite deadly sin: lust

portrait by Josh Gosfield

favorite deadly sin: sloth

Kent Hunter is Executive Design Director and a principal of Frankfurt Balkind Partners, an integrated communications agency based in New York and Los Angeles and San Francisco. Known for its innovative approach to annual reports, the firm is increasingly working in video and multi-media, utilizing their expertise in **advertising and entertainment marketing. The firm's work for Time Warner, MTV, The Limited,** MCI, and others has won every major design award. ∞ Kent is a past vice-president of the New York chapter of the American Institute of Graphic Arts, has judged numerous design shows and gives lectures around the country. He passionately collects folk art.

Kent **Hun**ter

Gail **Anders**on

Gail Anderson has worked at ''Rolling Stone'' with Fred Woodward since 1987, the past three years as deputy art director. She served as the assistant designer at ''The Boston Globe Magazine'' from 1985-87 and as a designer at **Vintage Books prior to that. Her work has received awards from the Society of Publication Designers, the Type Directors Club, AIGA, The Art Directors Club, and Communication Arts Magazine. She is co-author with Steven Heller of "Graphic Wit: The Art Of Humor in Design," and "The Savage Mirror: The Art of Contemporary Caricature." They are currently working together on "American Typography," a survey of modern type. A School of Visual Arts graduate, Gail now teaches design in SVA's Continuing Education program. Her work is represented in the permanent collection of the Cooper-Hewitt Design Resource and she serves on the Executive Committee of AIGA's New York chapter.**

favorite deadly sin: sloth

portrait by Robert **Risko**

favorite deadly sin: sloth

portrait by **Terry Allen**

Richard Baker was born in Kingston, Jamaica where he learned to Rub-A-Dub Style all night long to the tunes of **Big Youth. Faced with the career choices of working for the Royal Postal Service or selling kali weed, he headed no'th to The Big Apple. ∞ After graduating from the School of Visual Arts, he moved to Boston to work as a designer and art director for The Boston Globe. He then went to work for The Washington Post Magazine as its art director for three years. He is currently back in New York** working as art director at Vibe Magazine. ∞ He sometimes still thinks about a career in sales and postal service.

Richard Baker

Mark **Koudys**

Mark Koudys is Canadian, and therefore an extremely nice and polite person. He grew up in an octagonal house just outside Niagara Falls, which may or may not account for the many facets to his work and character today, but must **certainly explains his fear and loathing of tourism and honeymoons. Currently he is a principal of Atlanta Art and Design in Toronto, which specializes in editorial design and corporate communications programs. His work has been recognized by The American Institute for Graphic Arts, Society of Publica-** tion Designers, Communication Arts, Graphis and the Toronto Art Directors Club. His surname comes from Dutch parents, it's pronounced "cowt-ice," and it means "cold-ice," which raises the question of what other kind of ice they have in Holland...but perhaps it is not a question which need concern us any further here...

favorite deadly sin: lust

portrait by **Louis Fishauf**

favorite deadly sin: anger

Mirko Ilić was born in Bosnia in 1956. He started to publish his work at the age of seventeen. His work ranged from **comics and illustrations to art direction for film, theater posters, album covers and book covers. In 1986 he emigrated to the U.S. where he continued to work for a wide range of clients, primarily as an illustrator.** He has art directed "Time International" and is currently art directing the Op-Ed page of "The New York Times." Mirko has been awarded a gold medal by the Society of Illustrators and by the Society of Publication Designers.

Mirko Ilić

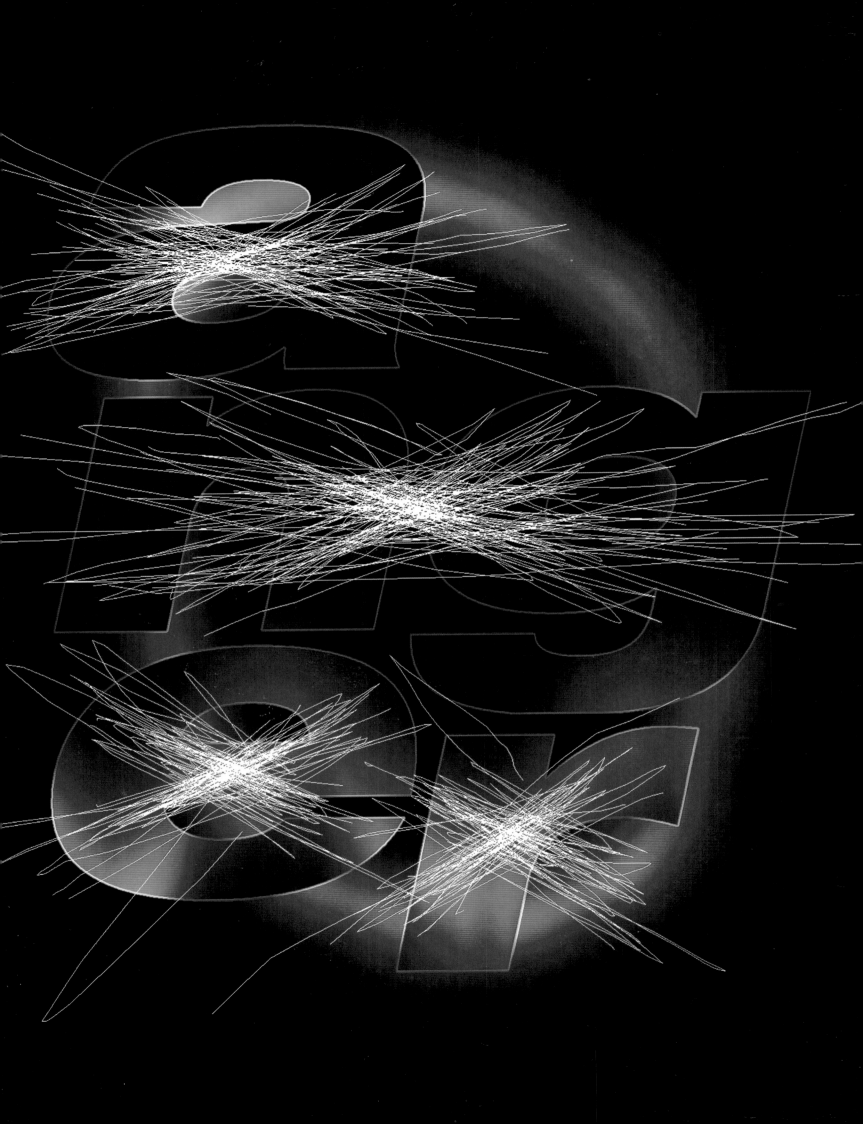

EDITORIAL

Barry Blitt

Art Directors) Chris Curry and Lee Lorenz Editor) Tina Brown Publication) The New Yorker Date) March 22, 1993
Publisher) Condé Nast Publications, Inc. Medium) Pen and ink, watercolor
Elvis Costello and the Brodsky Quartet as depicted for the feature "Goings on About Town."

17

Alexandra Weems

Art Director) Chris Curry Editor) Tina Brown **Publication) The New Yorker** Publisher) Condé Nast Publications, Inc.
Medium) Gouache on BFK Rives One of two **illustrations commissio**ned for The New Yorker's "Night Life" section.

Alexandra Weems

Art Director) Chris Curry   Editor) Tina Brown   Publication) The New Yorker   Publisher) Condé Nast Publications, Inc.
Medium) Gouache on BFK Rives   The second of two illustrations commissioned for The New Yorker's "Night Life" section (above).

∞

Art Director) Pamela Berry   Writer) Michael Kaplan   Publication) US Magazine   Date) August 1992   Publisher) Straight Arrow Publishers, Inc.
Medium) Gouache on paper   Cable sex shows were the subject of the article "You Get What You Pay For" featuring this illustration (right).

Maira Kalman

Blair Drawson

Art Director) Pamela Berry Publication) US Magazine Date) February 1992 Publisher) Straight Arrow Publishers, Inc.
Medium) Acrylic This image illustrated the article "What It's Like to be Gay in Hollywood."

Designer) Darrin Perry Editor) Chris Hunt Writer) Gary Smith Publication) Sports Illustrated Date) July 22, 1992. Publisher) The Time Inc. Magazine Company Medium) Pen and ink, dyes The unsophisticated American traveler is depicted here for the article "A Pain in Spain."

Maurice Vellekoop

(WITH APOLOGIES TO PIERRE AUGUSTE COT)

Edward Sorel

Art Director) Fred Woodward **Writer)** Peter Travers **Publication)** Rolling Stone
Date) October 1, 1992 **Publisher)** Straight Arrow Publishers, Inc. **Medium)** Pen and ink, watercolor
This parody **of** Pierre Cot's painting **accompanied the review of Wo**ody Allen's movie "Husbands and Wives."

Art **Directors)** Dwayne Flinchum **and Suzette Ruys Editor)** Bob Guccione   Writer) Kit Reed
Publication) Omni Magazine Date) March 1993 **Publisher)** **General Media** Publication Group   Medium) Oil on canvas
This illustration of a crazed woman being **chased by dogs was** created for the article "**Like** My Dress."

Sandra Hendler

Georganne Deen

Art Director) Judy Garlan Editor) Jack Beatty Writer) Wendy Kaminer Publication) The Atlantic Monthly
Date) November 1992 Publisher) The Atlantic Monthly Company Medium) AMIGA Computer/Diablo Printer
A critique of feminists' participation in the anti-pornography movement inspired this image.

Art Directors) Rudolph C. Hoglund **and Jane Frey** **Editor)** Johanna McGeary Writer) John Kohan
Publication) Russia **Special Issue of Time Magazine** **Date) December 7, 1992** Publisher) The Time Inc. Magazine Company
Medium) Paint and collage This collage accompanied the article "Can Russia Escape Its Past?"

Janet **Wo**olley

25

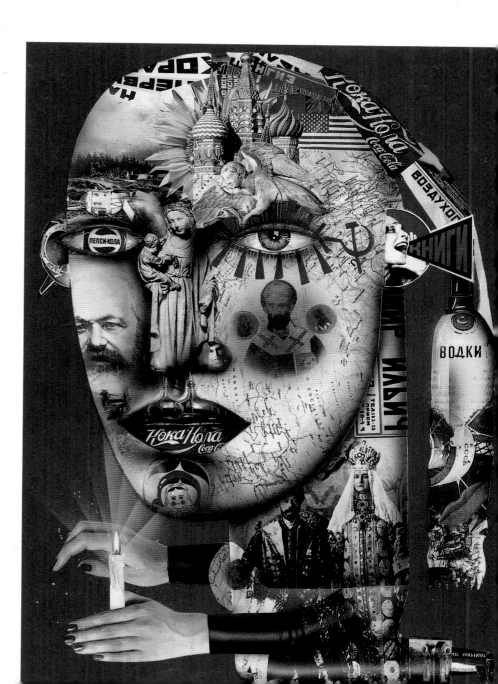

Art Director) Kerig Pope Designer) Tom **Staebler** **Writer)** Alex Haley Publication) Playboy Date) July 1992
Publisher) Playboy **Enterprises, Inc.** Medium) **Acrylic** **This illustration accompanied the article "Malcol**m X Remembered."

Brad **Holl**and

27

Edmund Guy

Art Director) Fred Woodward Writer) Mark Coleman **Publication) Rolling Stone** Date) November 26, 1992 Publisher) Straight Arrow Publishers, Inc. Medium) Collage The article **"Neneh's Hot 'Homebrew'"** featured this portrait of the singer Neneh Cherry.

Warren Linn

Art Director) Mirko Ilić Editor) David **Shipley** **Writer)** Ann **Mark**usen Publication) The New York Times
Date) November 22, **1992** Publisher) New York **Times Company** **Medium)** Collage and acrylic **This illust**ration accompanied
the article "Turning Off the **War Machine"** for the **Ne**w York Times Op-Ed page.

Step

Stephen Byram

Art Director) Mirko Ilić Editor) David Shipley Writer) T. Rosack Publication) The New York Times
Date) June 1992 Publisher) New York Times Company Medium) Mixed media This illustration accompanied
an essay on environmental and commerce issues for the Times Op-Ed page.

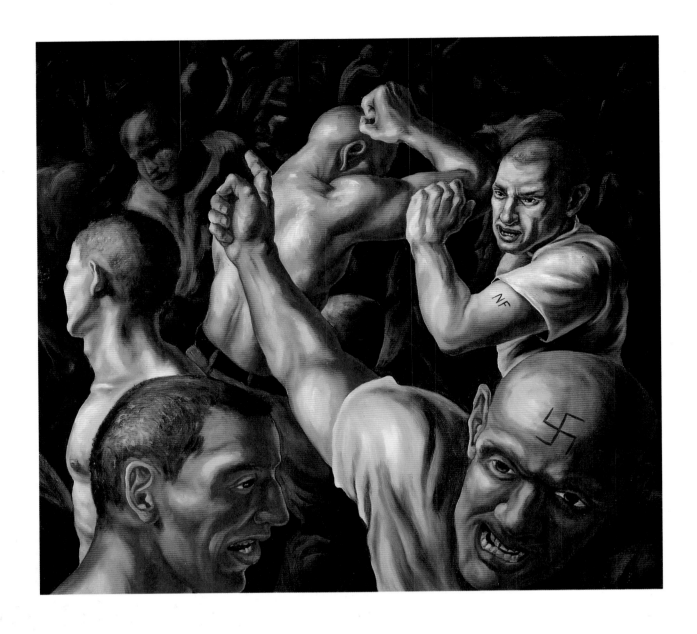

Owen Smith

Art Director) Janet Froelich Designer) Kandy Littrell Writer) Bill Buford Publication) The New York Times Magazine
Date) April 26, 1992 Publisher) New York Times Company Medium) Oil on board This illustration
depicts violent, chaotic dancing at an event organized by the National Front, a British Neo-Nazi group.

Art Director) Fred Woodward Publication) Rolling Stone Date) September 17, 1992
Publisher) Straight Arrow Publishers, Inc. Medium) Graphite and gouache Appearing on the Contents page,
this illustration ran with the heading "The Bush Years, Supreme Cruelty."

Sue Coe

Art Director) Fred Woodward **Publication) Rolling Stone** Date) September 3, 1992
Publisher) Straight Arrow Publishers, Inc. **Medium) Graphite and gouache** "The Bush Years, The Environmental President"
was the heading for this **illustration, appearing** on the Contents page.

Sue Coe

32

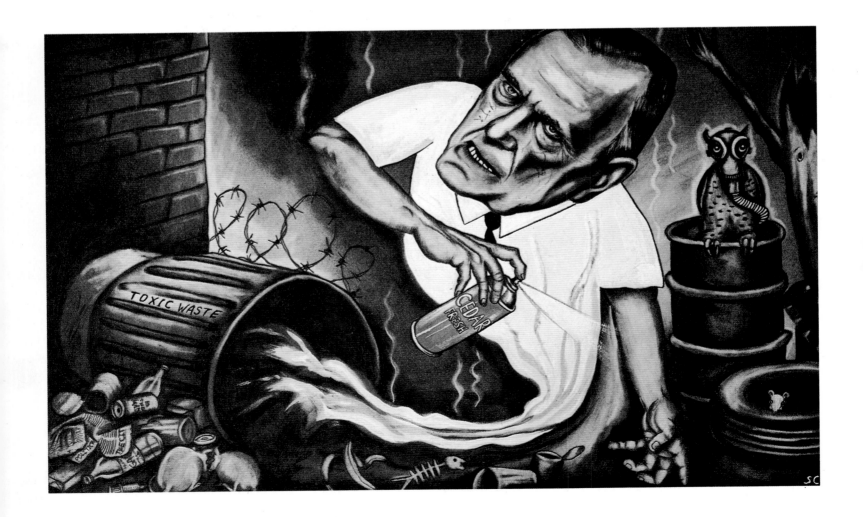

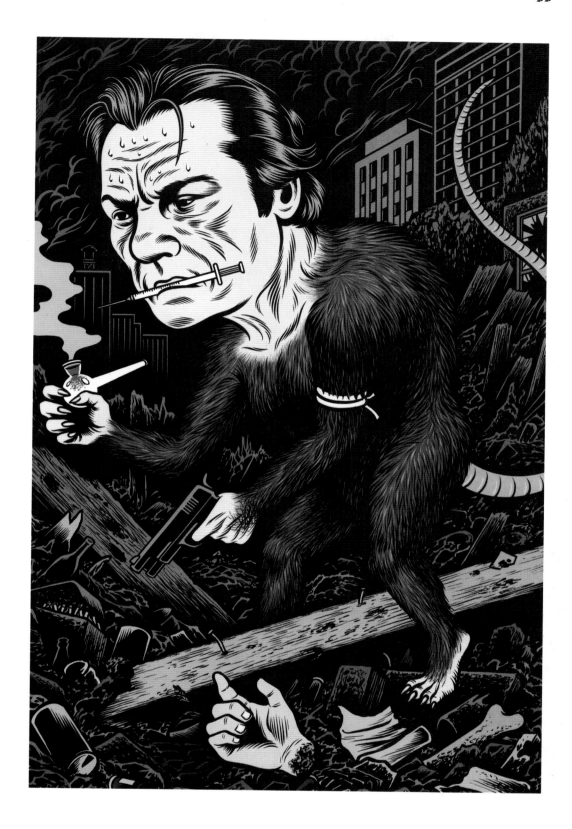

Charles Burns

Art Director) Fred Woodward Writer) Peter Travers **Publication) Rolling Stone** Date) November 26, 1992 Publisher) Straight Arrow Publishers, Inc. Medium) **Mixed media** A review of **"The Bad Lieutenant"** was accompanied by this depiction of its star, Harvey Keitel.

Charles Burns

Art Director) Chris Curry **Editor) Tina Brown Publication) The New Yorker**
Date) De**cember 14, 1992 Publisher) Condé Nast Publications, Inc.** Medium) **Pantone paper** and ink
This illustration was found in the "Night Life" section of The New Yorker (above).

∞

Art Director) Fred **Woodward Publication) Rolling Stone Date) October 15, 1992 Publisher) Straight Ar**row Publishers, Inc.
Medium) **Mixed media The 25th anniversary issue featured** this portrait of James Brown (right).

Art Director) Robert Priest   Writer) Steve Friedman   Publication) GQ Magazine   Date) February 1993
Publisher) Condé Nast Publications, Inc.   Medium) Mixed media   The question,
"Can sex put undue strain on your heart?" was asked in the feature "Personal Best."

Charles Burns

Gary **Base**man

Art Director) Susan Gockel Dazzo **Writer) Kathleen Clute** **Publication)** American Health Magazine
Date) April 1992 Publisher) **Reader's Digest Publications, Inc.** Medium) Mixed media
The article "**Mighty Sperm From Little Acorns**" discusses the potency of sperm with acorn shaped heads.

David **Hug**hes

Art Director) Richard **Baker** Designer) Kelly Doe **Editor) Bob Thompson** Writer) Peter Carlson Publication) The Washington
Post Magazine Date) July 26, 1992 **Publisher) The Washington** Post Company Medium) **Gouache a**nd ink
"When **Henry Met Zsa Zsa,**" a humor**ous look at celebrity auto**biographies, featured this illustra**ti**on.

Art Director) Charles Churchward   Writer) Anthony Summers   Publication) Vanity Fair
Date) March 1993   Publisher) Condé Nast Publications, Inc.   Medium) Gouache   This illustration ran
with the article "Hidden Hoover," which revealed one of his more interesting pastimes.

Robert Risko

Steve Brodner

Art Director) Pamela Berry Publication) US **Magazine Date) March 19**93 Publisher) Straight Arrow Publishers, Inc.
Medium) Mixed **media using computer The caricature of Jack Nichol**son highlights the actor's features (above).

∞

Art Director) Adam Smith Publication) **Mirabella Date) April** 1993 Publisher) Murdoch Publications
Medium) Mixed media using computer **This caricature of Sol Wach**tler was created with the computer (left).

42

Ralph Steadman

Art Director) **Fred Woodward** Writer) **Hunter S. Thompson** Publication) **Rolling Stone** Date) **January** 23, 1992
Publisher) Straight Arrow Publishers, Inc. Medium) **Mixed media The article** "Fear and Loathing in ELKO" featured this image.

Art Director) Lisa Powers Editor) Kenneth Auchincloss Writers) Steven Strasser, Bill Powell, Peter McKillop, Frank Gibney Jr., George Wehrfritz Publication) Newsweek International Date) December 21, 1992 Publisher) The Washington Post Company Medium) Linoleum cut The quest for democracy in Asia is represented in this illustration for the article "People Power."

Frances Jetter

43

Art Director) Jane Palecek Editor) Eric Schrier Writer) David Sharp Publication) Health Date) April 1992
Publisher) Hippocrates Partners Medium) Acrylic The article "Send in the Crowds" was accompanied by this illustration.

Blair Drawson

Art Director) Joan Ferrell Editor) Deborah Wilburn Writer) Paula M. Siegel Publication) Working Mother Magazine Date) January 1993
Publisher) Lang Communications Medium) Pastel **The painful consequences** of a child's shame are depicted in this image.

Wiktor **Sado**wski

Jordin Isip

Art Director) David Carson Editor) Marvin Scott Jarrett **Publication) Ray Gun** Date) April 1993 **Publisher)** Ray Gun Publishing, Inc.
Medium) Mixed media **An interpretation of the song "Breadcrumb Trail" by the** Slint band for the feature "Sound in Print" (above).

∞

Art Director) **Kate Thompson** Editor) M**. Mark Writer) Erik Davis** Publication) Voice Literary Supplement
Date) March 1993 **Publisher)** VV Publishing **Corporation Medium) Mixed** media "A Computer, A Universe," an article
which e**xplored the possibilities of an online cosmological pro**gram, included this **illustrati**on (left).

Art Director) Laura N. Frank Editor) Earl W. Foell Writer) Zbigniew Brzezinski
Publication) World Monitor Magazine Date) March 1993 Publisher) The Christian Science Publishing Society
Medium) Mixed-media This illustration accompanied the article entitled "Power and Morality."

Jordin Isip

David **Plunk**ert

Art D**irector)** Mark Evans   Editor) **Jim Duffy   Writer) Kevin** Whitehead   Publication) City **P**aper
Date) February 12, 1993   Publisher) **Scranton Times   Medium)** C**o**llage, pen and ink, graphite **a**nd coffee
"Joined at th**e Hip, Berlin Does Believe in Tears,"** an article **about** German reunification, featured this image.

David Plunkert

Art Director) Leigh Caruso Writer) Patricia A. Galagan Publication) Training and Development Magazine
Date) March 1993 Publisher) American Society for Training and Development Medium) Collage
Race role reversal at a chemical plant was the subject of the article "Trading Places at Monsanto."

David Plunkert

Art Director) Leigh Caruso Writer) Patricia A. Galagan Publication) Training and Development Magazine
Date) March 1993 Publisher) American Society for Training and Development Medium) Collage
One of three illustrations for the feature "Navigating the Differences/Special Report on Diversity."

Da**vid Pl**unk**e**rt

Art Director) Leigh **Caruso** Writer) John **Dovidio** **Publication) Training** **and** Development **Magazine** Date) March 1993
Publisher) American **Society for Training and Development** **Medium) Collage** The article "Denying Racism" inspired this collage.

Art Director) Jane Palecek   Editor) Eric Schrier   Writer) Edward Dolnick   Publication) Health
Date) July/August 1992   Publisher) Hippocrates Partners   Medium) Mixed media
The characteristics of pathological liars inspired this illustration for the article "The Great Pretender."

Josh Gosfield and Nola Lopez

Art Director) Laura N. Frank Editor) Earl W. Foell Writer) Stephen H. Schneider Publication) World Monitor Magazine
Date) April 1993 Publisher) Christian Science Publishing Society Medium) Mixed media Teaching children creative thinking
was the subject of the article "A Better Way to Learn" featuring these two illustrations.

Christian Northeast

Art Director) Pamela Berry Writer) Jeffrey Ressner Publication) US Magazine Date) March 1993 Publisher) Straight Arrow Publishers, Inc.
Medium) Mixed media Hollywood's use of audience polling to predict the success of films was the subject of this illustration.

Christian Northeast

Maris BIshofs

Art Director) Michele Chu Editor) David Gergen Writer) Steve Anderson Publication) U.S. News & World Report
Date) October 26, 1992 Publisher) World Color Press Medium) Ink and watercolor The problems that judges and juries face
struggling with complex scientific testimony gave rise to this illustration.

Brian Cronin

Art Director) Martin Colyer Editor) **Steve Weinman Writers)** Eric Waugh, Keith Graves, Jon Devitt,
Charles Scanlon and Fergal Keane Publication) BBC Worldwide Date) January 1993
Medium) Pen and ink, watercolor The BBC **Worldwide Report article** "Borders" gave rise to this illustration.

Art Director) Joseph Dizney Editor) Stuart Emmrich Writer) James Lyons Publication) Smart Money Date) April 1993
Publisher) Hearst & Dow Jones Medium) Watercolor The article "Is Your Bank Ripping You Off?" featured this illustration.

Jeffrey Fisher

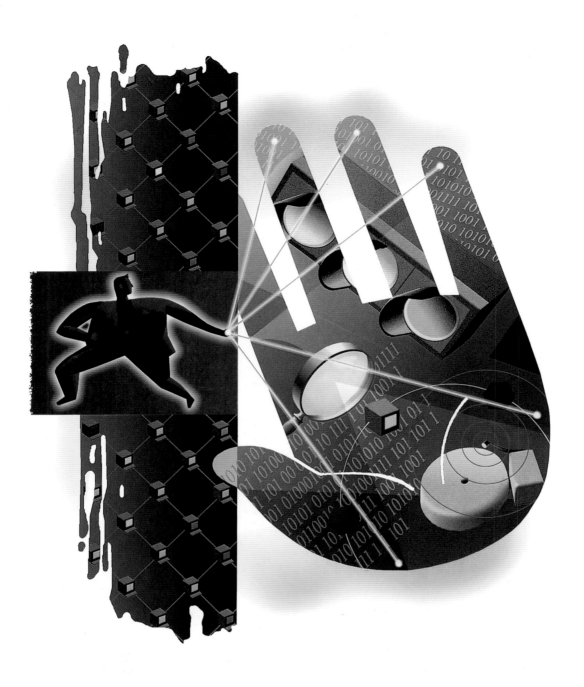

Mick **WIgg**ins

Art Di**rect**or) Joanne Hoffman Write**r) Shelly Brisbin Publica**tion) Macworld Date) **February** 1993
Publisher) Macworld **Communications, Inc. Mediu**m) **Computer This illustra**tion accompanied the article "Network Utilities,"
a guide to the best tools f**or diagnosing and solving** computer network problems.

Art **Director)** David Armario **Writer) Spyros Andreopoulos** Publication) Stanford Medicine
Date) Fall 1992 **Publisher)** Stanford University Medical Center Office of Communications Medium) Gouache
Peptic ulcers were discussed in the article "The internal Flame," featuring this image.

Terry Allen

61

Hanoch Piven

Art Director) Chris Curry Editor) Tina Brown Publication) The New Yorker Date) March 29, 1993 Publisher) Condé Nast Publications, Inc.
Medium) Gouache and sandpaper This caricature of pop singer Prince was included in the feature "Goings on About Town" (below).

∞

Art Directors) Fred Woodward and Gail Anderson Writer) Peter Travers Publication) Rolling Stone
Date) February 4, 1993 Publisher) Straight Arrow Publishers, Inc. Medium) Collage
"Madonna's Come-On," a review of her movie "Body of Evidence," included this caricature (right).

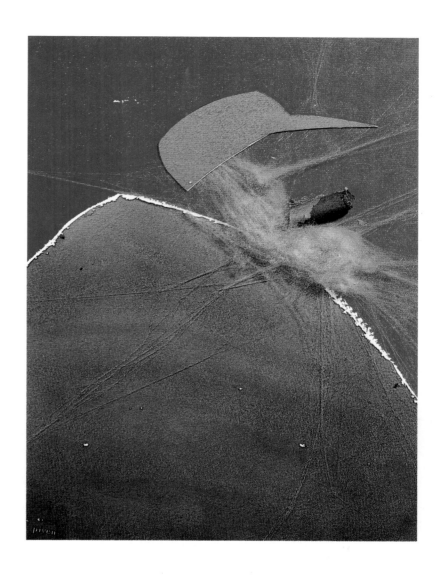

Hanoch Piven

Medium) Collage This caricature of Fidel Castro previously unpublished (above).

∞

Design Director) Michael Grossman Art Director) Elizabeth Betts Writer) Ken Tucker Publication) Entertainment Weekly
Date) January 7, 1993 Publisher) The Time Inc. Magazine Company Medium) Gouache and Oreos
This caricature of Roseanne Arnold is from the "1992 Best and Worst" feature in Entertainment Weekly (left).

Art Director) Fred Woodward Writer) Grant Alden Publication) Rolling Stone
Date) January 21, 1993 Publisher) Straight Arrow Publishers, Inc. Medium) Collage, pencil, acrylic and photo transfer
This illustration accompanied a review of rock music entitled "The Remains of Grunge."

Brian **Krue**ger

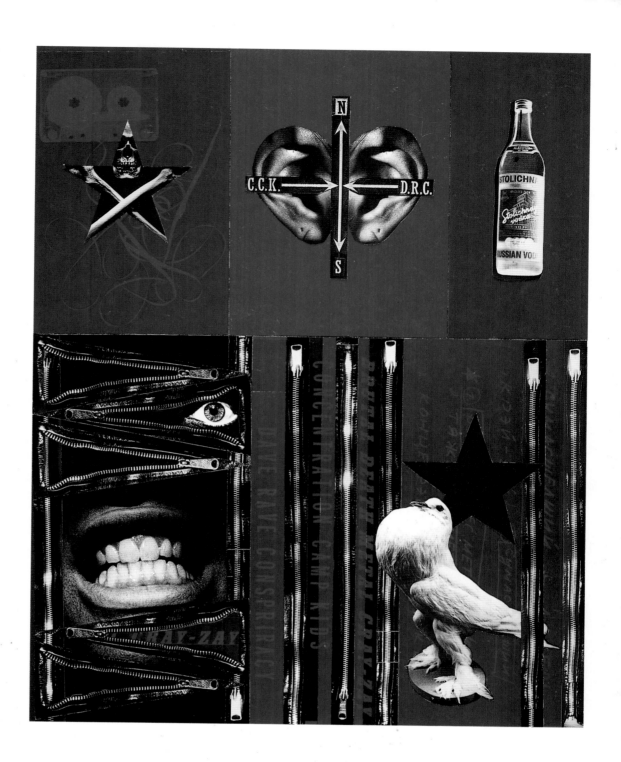

Amy Guip

Art Director) David **Carson** Editor) Marvin **Scott Jarrett** Writer) Lauren Agnelli Publication) Ray Gun Date) March 1993
Publisher) Ray Gun Publishing, Inc. Medium) Collage This illustration was created for the article "Recording in Soviet Dis-Union."

Amy Guip

Art Director) Da**vid Carson** Editor) Marvin **Scott Jarrett Writer) Dave Allen** Publication) **Ray Gun** Date) April 1993
Publisher) Ray Gun **P**ublishing, Inc. Medium) Mix**ed media The Ray Gun f**eature "Pop Smear" included th**e**se two illustrations.

Gary **Tanhau**ser

Art **Director)** Jane Palecek Ed**itor)** Eric Sch**rier** **Writer)** **Bo**nnie Wach Publication) He**a**lth
Date) September **1992** Publisher) Hippocrate**s** **Partners** **Medium) Mixed** media **The task of choosin**g a unique name
for **your** child was the subject **of "What's in a Name,"** f**e**aturing this illustration (abov**e**).

∞

Art Director**)** **Pat Mitchell** Writer) Bill B**reen** **Publication) Garbage** Magazine Date) December/January 1993
Publisher) Dovetale Publishe**rs** Medium) Mixed media **This image was created for** an editorial about cons**u**mer product packaging (left).

Art Director) Claude Skelton Editor) Jim Rice Writer) Robert Heilbroner Publication) Washington Monthly
Date) February 1993 Publisher) Capital City Publications Medium) Collage This collage ran with the article
"Waiting for Change, What Can We Expect From the Clinton Administration?"

David Plunkert

Art Director) Roger **Black** Editor) Terry McDonell **Writer) Jim Harrison Publication)** Esquire **Sportsman** Date) Autumn 1992
Publisher) The Hearst **Corporation** Medium) Oil **This illustration accompanie**d the article "A New Map of the Sacred Territory."

Ben̂oît

Ben̂oît

Brian Cronin

Art Director) Lucy **Bartholomay** Editor) Ande **Zellman Writer) Anita Diam**ant Publication) **The Boston** Globe Magazine
Date) **March 14, 1993** Publisher) **Affiliated Publications, Inc. M**edium) Pen and ink and wat**e**rcolor
The cover illustration for **the feature "What's the M**atter with Men?" (above).

∞

Art Director) David Lo**e**wy Editor) **Florence Lazar Publication) Varbusiness** Date) February 1993 **Publish**er) CMP Publications
Medium) Collage **This interpretation of the g**l**obal salesman was use**d for the article "Sales Around the World" (left).

David **Plunk**ert

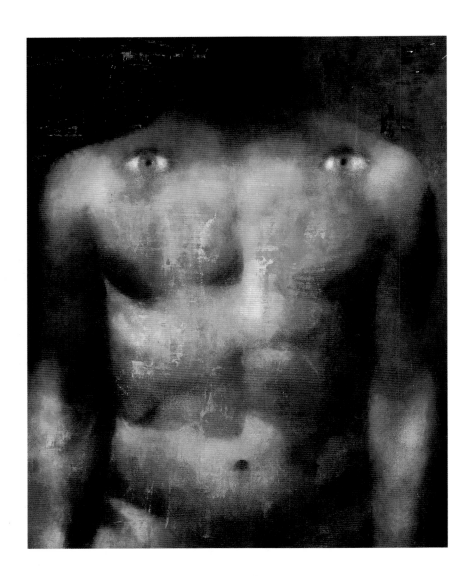

Brad **Holl**and

Art Director) **John Sanford** Publication) TLC **Monthly Date) January 19**93 Publisher) Discovery Communications Medium) Acrylic **This image was used as the cover for the feature "**Body and Soul, Between Synap**se and Psyche."

Art Director) Chuck Routhier **Editor) Daniel Ruby** Writer) **Eliot Bergson Publication)** NeXTWORLD **Date) Fall 199**2 Publisher) Integrated Media
Medium) Collage This image illustrates NeXT's approach to **build-it-yourself** programming for the automation of business processes.

Mal**colm Tarlof**sky

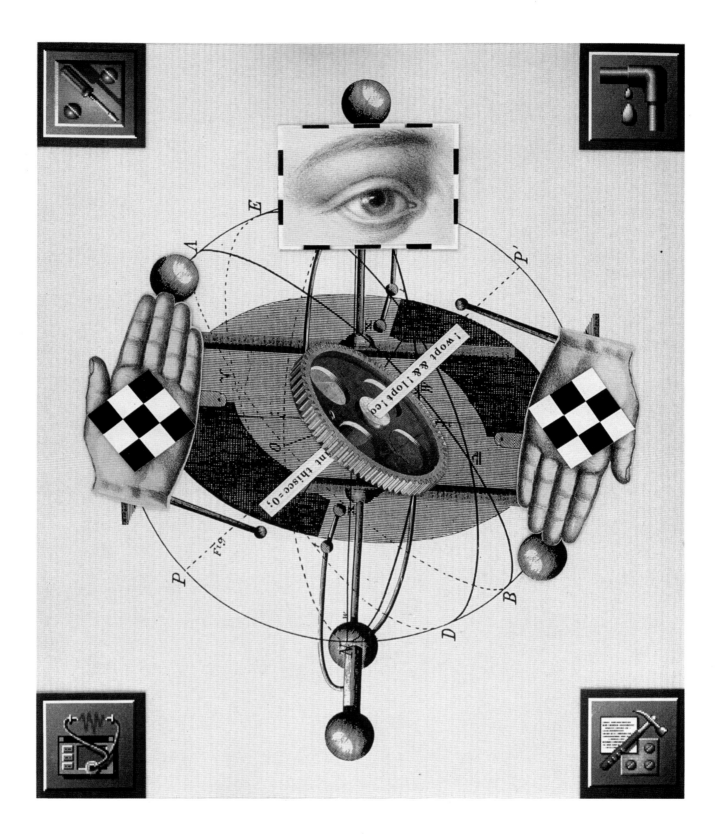

Eric DInyer

Art Director) David Carson Editor) **Marvin Scott Jarrett Publi**cation) Ray Gun Date) March 1993
Publi**sher)** Ray Gun Publishing, Inc. **Medium) Paint, photog**raphy and computer manipulation
Evan **Lurie's song "Alfredo's Respons**e" **was interpreted for the** Ray Gun feature "Sound in Print."

Art Director) Jane Palecek Editor) Eric Schrier Writer) **Edward Dolnick Publication**) Health Date) **July/August** 1992 Publisher) Hippocrates Partners Medium) Photograph **This illustration was created for the article "The Great Pretender,"** an examination of pathological liars.

Matt **Mahur**in

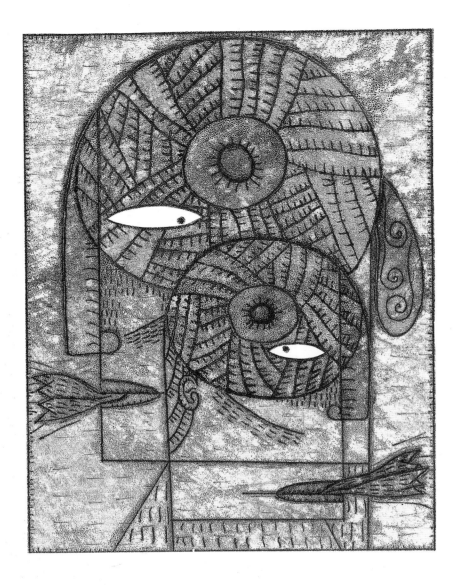

Richard Downs

Art Directors) Fred Woodward and Gail Anderson Writer) Scott Isler Publication) Rolling Stone
Date) February 4, 1993 Publisher) Straight Arrow Publishers, Inc. Medium) Mixed media
A review of Stiff and Chiswick's recent CD containing early punk music was accompanied by this illustration.

Editors) Sandy Jimenez, **Sabrina Jones and Seth Tob**ocman   Writer) José Ortega
Publication) **World War Three**   Date) **January 1993   Medium) Scratch**board and copier   "**Invasion!!!**," a study of
the European and North American inva**sion of Latin America fro**m 1492 to 1992, featured this illustration.

José **Ort**ega

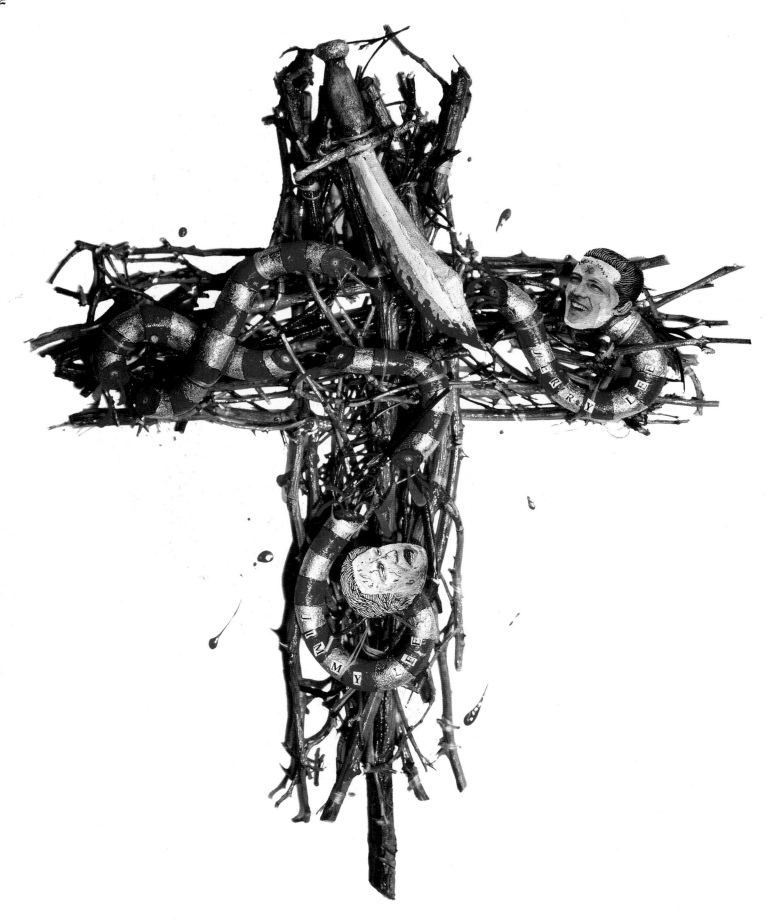

Henrik Drescher

Art Director) Fred Woodward Writer) Lawrence Wright Publication) Rolling Stone Date) June 11, 1992 Publisher) Straight Arrow
Publishers, Inc. Medium) Mixed media The article "False Messiah," a look at Jimmy Swaggart, featured this illustration.

Jason **Holley**

Art Di**rector)** Tom Fillebrown Edit**or) Marc Weidenbaum Writer)** Mike Gitter Publication)** Pulse!
Date) October **1992 Publisher)** MTS Inc. **Medium) Mixed media** **"Everything You Ever** Wanted to Know About
Death Metal, but Were Afraid to **Ask," was the title of the** article featuring this illustration.

84

Joel **Peter John**son

Art Directors) Dwayne **Flinchum** and Suzette Ru**ys** **Editor) Bob Guccione** **Writer)** Marc Laidlaw **Publicati**on) Omni Magazine
Date) May 1993 Publisher) **General Media Publication Group Medium) Acrylic and** oil The quote "It's **wonderf**ul to see darkness again,"
taken from "The Diane Arbus **Suicide Portfolio," is the ba**sis for this haunting **illustrati**on.

Art Director) **Kerry Tremain** Writer) **Veronique Vienne Publication)** Mother Jones Magazine Dat**e) March 1993
Publisher) Foundation fo**r National Progress Medium) Acrylic A mother searche**s for her son in the article "Iron John: A Love Story."

Brad **Holla**nd

Patrick Blackwell

Art Director) Lucy Bartho**lomay** **Editor)** Ande Zellman. Writer) John R. Stilgoe
Publication) The Boston **Globe** Magazine Date) July **5, 1992** **Publisher)** **Affiliate**d Publications, Inc. Medium) Wood, ink and gouache
This illustration ac**companied the article "Woo**d **Stock," a history and appreciation of the New England** building shingle.

Art Director) Rhonda Rubinstein Editor) Terry McDonell Writer) Peter Maas Publication) Esquire Date) January 1992 Publisher) Hearst Corporation Medium) Acrylic "Lawyers, Guns, and Money" featured this illustration in Esquire's Dubious Achievement issue.

Jeffrey Fisher

87

Rick **Sea**lock

Art Director) Claire Innes Editor) Rick Sylvain **Writer) Melinda Beck Publication)** Detroit Free Press Date) August 16, 1992
Publisher) Knight-Ridder Medium) Watercolor, acrylic, **pastel and collage This illustration was created for** the Sunday Travel Section
article "At Home on the Range," **a story about an all-wo**men, out-west vacation ranch.

Art Director) David Carson Editor) Marvin Scott Jarrett Publication) Ray Gun Date) November 1992 Publisher) Ray Gun Publishing, Inc.
Medium) Mixed media For the feature "Sound in Print" this image represents the illustrator's favorite song, "Ring of Fire" by Johnny Cash.

Christian Clayton

LAST AND FINAL ROUND OF THE PRESIDENTIAL DEMOLITION DERBY.
LADIES AND GENTS, IN THE LEFT CORNER WE SEE THE CHALLENGER, A WOBBLY, EGO-PROPELLED CAMPAIGN MACHINE
1/2 FULL
1/2 EMPTY
COLLISION COURSE
EXCESS PERSONAL BAGGAGE
JERRY B.
CENTER FIELD
ON THE RIGHT IS THE TIRED BUT DETERMINED INCUMBENT
FOREIGN OIL INTAKE
DANNY
OLD WIND-BAG
BOTTOMLESS PIT OF NAT'L DEBT
EYE-BALL OF THE NATION
TRIBAL SPIN DOCTOR
PARTY HACKS
PARTY CRASHER
'92 J.ROSEN
KEY:
A. CRUMBLING NATURE SUBSTITUTE
B. MONEY INTAKE VALVE
C. COMPLICATED PARTY PLATFORM
D. INFLAMMATORY ORATION
E. EVIDENCE OF SCANDAL
F. SAME OLD TIRED IDEAS, SAME OLD FINGER POINTING
G. URBAN MELTDOWN
H. THE BOY IN THE BUBBLE
I. EMPTY PARTY PLATFORM
J. WILD PUNCHING TECHNIQUE
K. ADVISERS, YES-MEN, POLLSTERS, AND LOBBYISTS
L. THE WILD CARD AND
M. HIS MONEY
THE END.

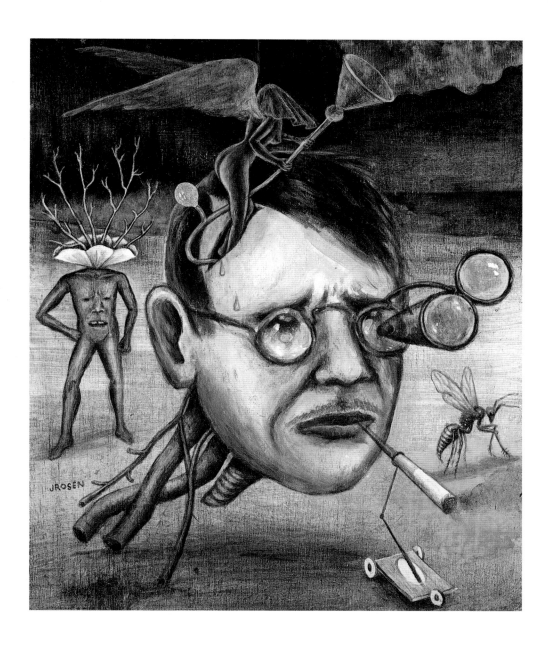

Jonathon Rosen

Art Director) David Carson Editor) Marvin **Scott Jarrett Publication) Ra**y Gun Date) **Fall 1992 Pu**blisher) Ray Gun Publishing, Inc. **Medium) Acrylic An interpretation of the song "Love**'s Secret Domain" by the gro**up Co**il (above).

∞

Art Director) B.W. **Honeycutt Publication) Details Date) August 199**3 Publisher) Condé Nast Publications, Inc. Medium) Acrylic **The pre-presidential election battle is** depicted in this illustration (left).

Brad **Holl**and

Art Director) Fred Woodward Publication) Rolling **Stone** **Date) October 15,** 1992 Publisher) **Straight Arr**ow Publishers, Inc.
Medium) Acrylic on m**asonite** **This portrait of Ra**y **Charles was included in the** 25th anniversary issue article "The Interviews."

Janet **Wo**olley

Art Director) Fred Woodward   Publication) Rolli**ng Stone   Date) October 15,** 1992   Publisher) Straight Arrow Publishers, Inc.
Medium) Mixed **media   This portrait of Jerry Garcla appeared in the 25**th anniversary issue article "The Interviews."

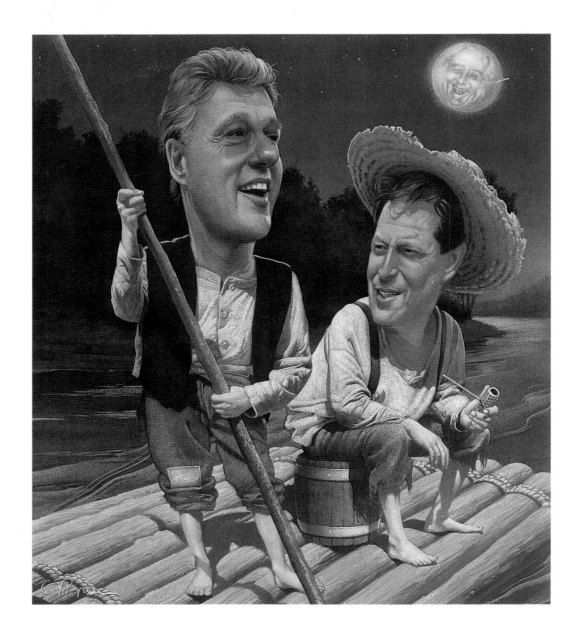

C.F. **Pay**ne

Art Director) Robert Priest **Writer) John Mortimer Publication) GQ Magazine Da**te) April 1993 Publisher) **Condé** Nast Publications, Inc.
Medium) Mixed **media The perplexities of being Princess DI were dicuss**ed in the article "Nobles**se** Besieged" (above).

∞

Art Director) Robert Priest **Writer) Gore Vidal Publication) GQ Magazine Date)** November 1992 Publisher) **Condé** Nast Publications, Inc.
Medium) Mixed media Clinton **and Gore are depicted here f**or the article "Goin' South" (left).

Warren Linn

Art Directors) Victoria Maddocks and **Jaime Ferrand** **Editor)** Katherine Arthaud Writer) Stan Gibilisco
Publication) South Beach Magazine Date) **February 1993** **Publisher)** South Beach Magazine, Inc. Medium) Collage and
acrylic on wood **A family at home with a polluted ocean was created** for the article "Earthwatch: Seawise" (below).

∞

Art Director) Nancy Duckworth **Editor)** Bret Israel **Publication)** The Los Angeles Times Magazine
Date) April 18, 1993 Publisher) Times **Mirror** **Medium)** **Oil and acrylic** A portrait of African American
men and women was **created for the article "Sh**ades of Black" (right).

Calef Brown

Sandra Dionisi

Art Director) Tom Suzuki Designer) Tim Cook Writers) William E. Winter and Mark A. Atkinson
Publication) Diabetes Forecast Date) May 1992 Publisher) American Diabetes Association, Inc.
Medium) Acrylic This illustration depicts the connection between diabetes and DNA.

Art Director) Tom Suzuki Designer) Tim Cook **Writer) Leslie R. Schover** Publication) Diabetes Forecast Date) August 1992
Publisher) American Diabetes Association Medium) Oil **on wood The article "Wo**men, Sexual Health and Diabetes" inspired this illustration.

Stefano Vitale

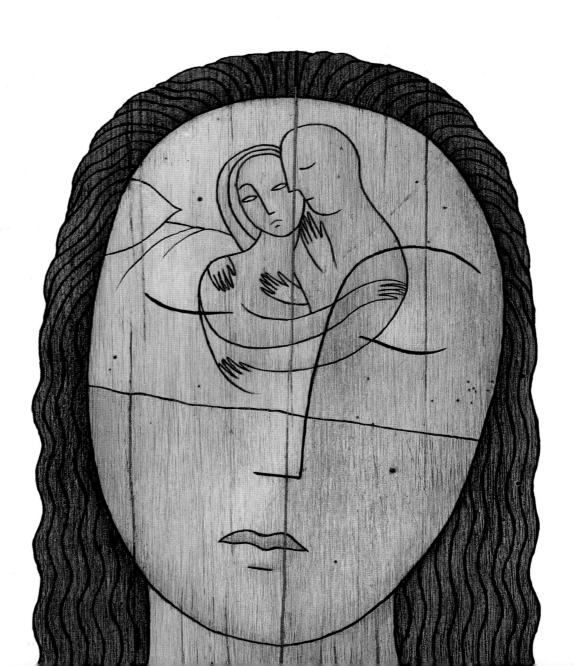

100

José Ortega

Art Director) Jessica Helfand Editor) Avery Rome Writer) Louis J. Rodriguez Publication) Philadelphia Inquirer Magazine
Date) February 21, 1993 Publisher) Knight-Ridder Medium) Pencil, copier and cut paper This illustration accompanied the article
"Trapped in the Land of the Free," about a Mexican family and their experiences in the United States.

Art Director) **Sarah Stearns** Editor) **William Inman** **Writer) Douglas C.** McGill Publication) **Bloom**berg Magazine
Date) **November 1992** Publisher) **Michael Bloomberg Publish**ing Medium) **Ink and water**color
"**Japan's** Newest Invention**"** **was the title of an article** featuring this image.

Phi**lippe Lar**dy

Art Director) Mark Koudys   Editor) Betty Ewing-Pearse   Publication) Digital News   Date) Spring 1993
Publisher) Digital Equipment of Canada, Ltd.   Medium) Pen and ink, watercolor, and collage
This illustration charts the evolution of the business enterprise, from supplier to business partner.

Barry Blitt

PHILIPPE WEISBECKER

Philippe Weisbecker

Art Director) Chris Sloane Writer) Dan Moreau Publication) Kiplinger's Personal Finance Magazine Date) June 1992
Publisher) Kiplinger Washington Editors Medium) Watercolor The article "Investments That Won't Let You Down" featured this illustration.

Jonath**on** **Ros**en

Art Directors) David **Armario and James Lambertus** **Editors) Paul Hoffman a**nd Patricia Gadsby Writer) Jerold M. Lowenstein
Publication) Discover Ma**gazine** Date) December 199**2 Publisher) Disney Magazi**ne Publishing, Inc. Medium) Acrylic and pen and ink
The seriously weird things **that are popping out of our DNA were discussed in "Ge**netic Surprises," which **featur**ed these two illustrations.

Michael Bartalos

Art Director) Linda Birch Editor) Bob O'Donnell Writers) Larry Oppenheimer and Scott Wilkinson Publication) Electronic Musician
Date) March 1993 Publisher) Act III Publishing Medium) Cut paper This Illustration was created for the article "The Digital Puzzle."

Art Director) **Cindy Hoffman** Editor) **Gail Ravgiala Writer) Ellen Steinbaum** Publication) **The** Boston Globe
Date) April 25, 1993 **Publisher) Affiliated Publications, Inc. Medium) Mixed** media "**The Resilient Ones,**" an article examining
the factors **that allow children to survive dysfunctional upbringings,** was accompanied by **this** illustration.

Steven **Guarnacc**ia

107

gli occhiali di Le Corbusier

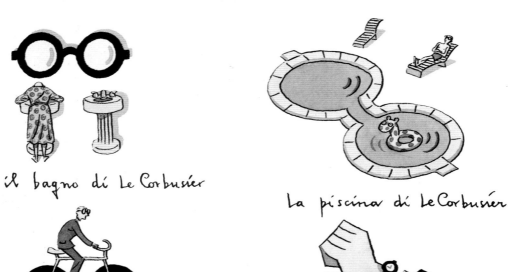

il bagno di Le Corbusier

la piscina di Le Corbusier

la bicicletta di
Le Corbusier

L'orologio di
Le Corbusier

la musica di Le Corbusier

il biliardo di Le Corbusier

Steven Guarnaccia

Art Director) Silvia Latis Editor) Renato Minetto Publication) Abitare Date) May 1992 Publisher) Abitare Segesta Medium) Ink and water
This illustration, entitled "Le Corbusier's Eyeglasses," was commissioned for an Italian magazine.

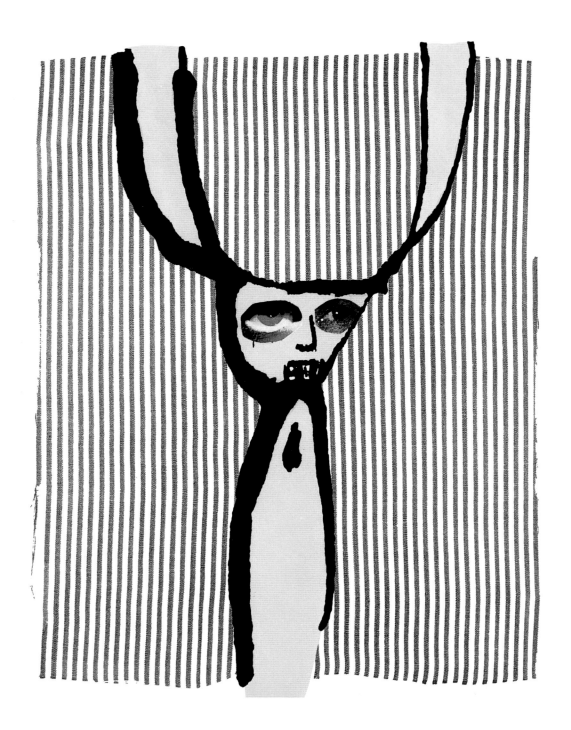

109

Scott Menchin

Art Director) Richard Baker Designer) Kelly Doe Editor) Bob Thompson Writer) Susan Cohen
Publication) The Washington Post Magazine Date) January 1993 Publisher) The Washington Post Company
Medium) Ink and collage "Tie Guy" accompanied the article entitled "White Collar Blues."

Art Director) Kate Thompson Writer) Henry Louis Gates Jr. Publication) The Village Voice Date) October 20, 1992
Publisher) VV Publishing Corporation Medium) Ink This illustration accompanied the article "Memoirs of an Anti-Anti-Semite."

Scott Menchin

110

111

Frances Jetter

Art Director) Jennifer Gilman Writer) Elizabeth Ho Publication) The Village Voice Date) May 19, 1992 Publisher) VV Publishing Corporation
Medium) Linoleum cut The debate over abortion rights was the subject of "Packaging Prochoice," which featured this illustration.

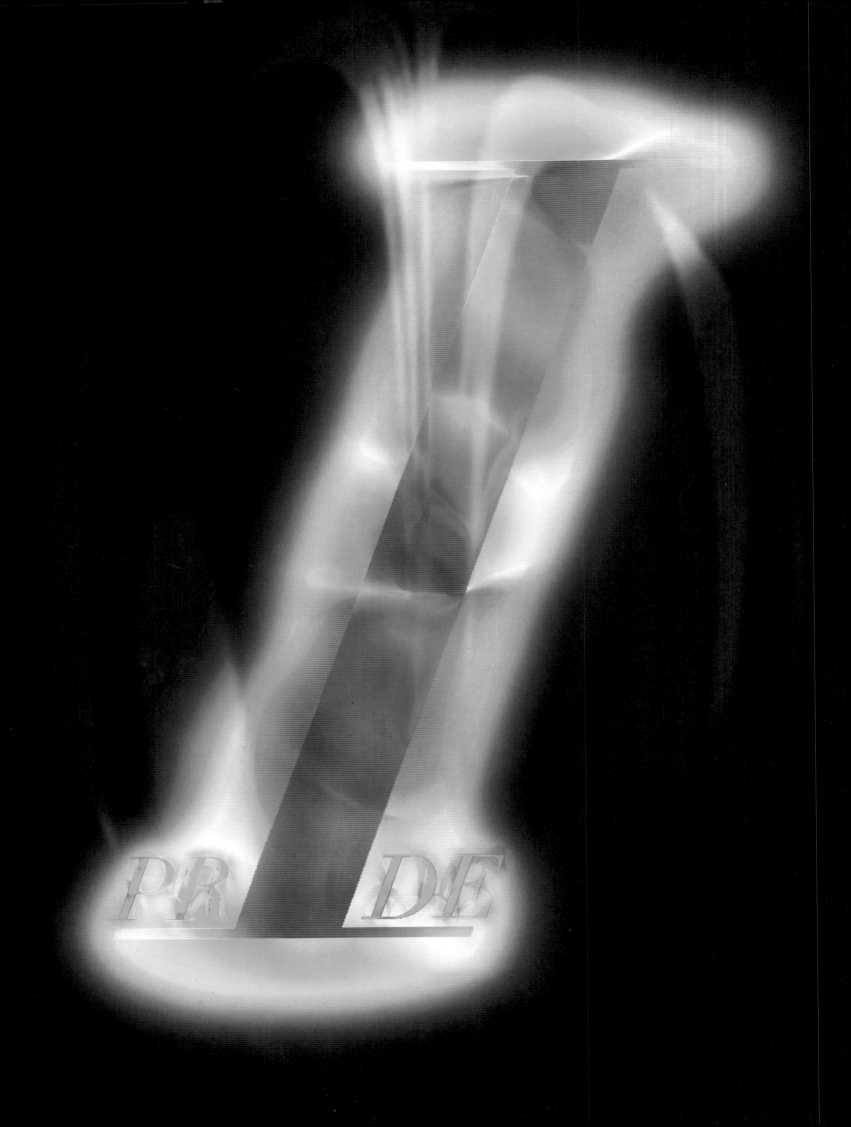

BOOKS

David Diaz

Art Director) Cecelia Diaz Designer) David Diaz Date) December 1992 Publisher) Icon Books Medium) Ink
This series of three-dimensional images was created for the book "Sweet Peas."

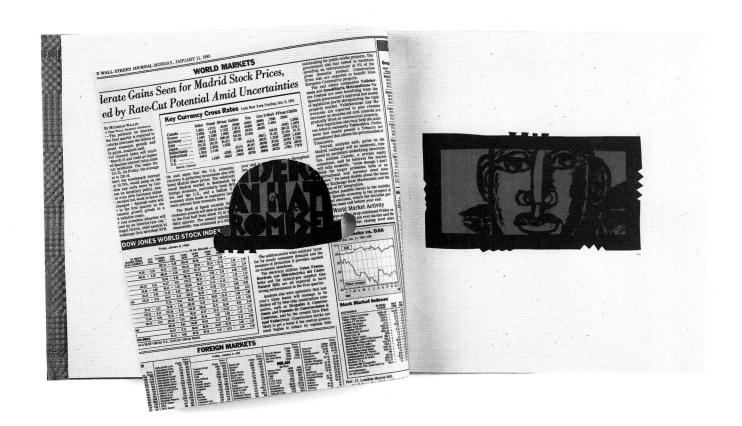

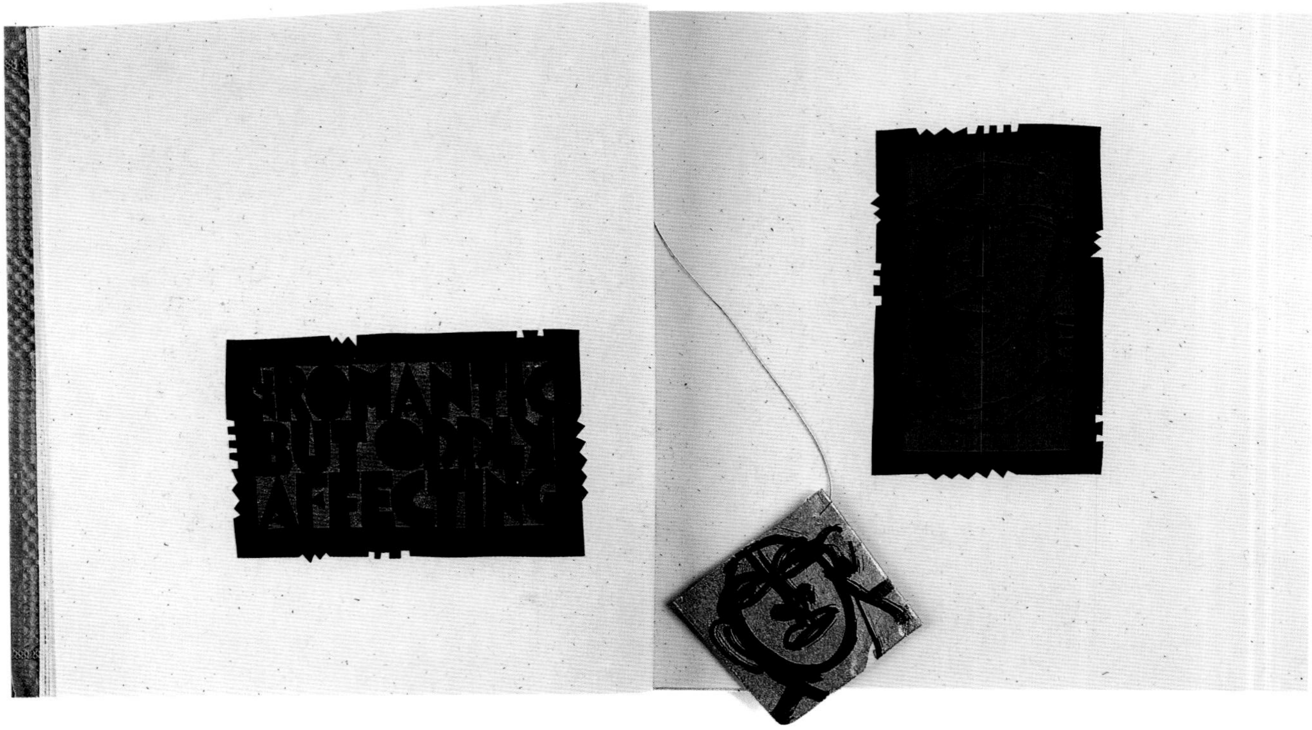
ROMANTIC
BUT ODDLY
AFFECTING

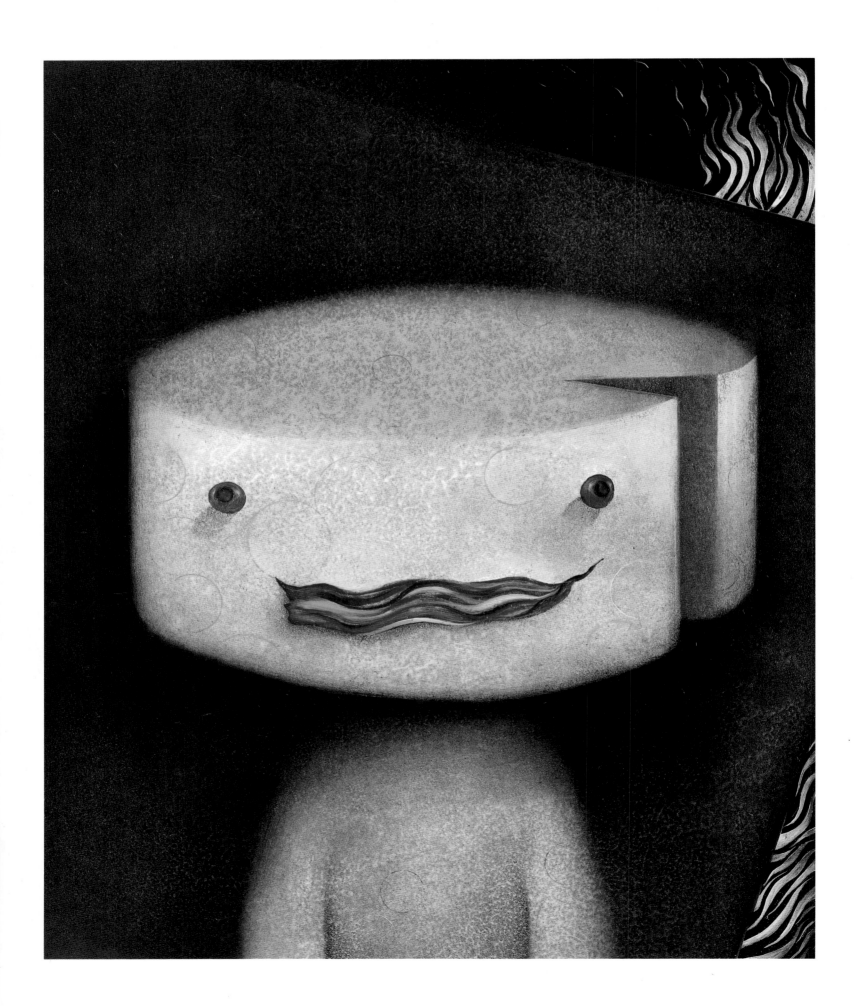

Lane **S**mith

Art Director) Molly Leach Editor) Regina Hayes Writer) **Jon Scieszka Date) 1993** Publisher) Viking Books Medium) Mixed media These four illustrations appear in the book **"The Stinky Cheese Man and Other Fairly Stupid Tales."** This one introduces "The Stinky Cheese Man" (left).

∞

"Jack's Story" (above).

"Chicken Licken"

"The Really Ugly Duckling"

J. Otto Seibold

Writers) J. Otto Seibold and Vivian Walsh Date) 1993 Publisher) Viking Books Medium) Macintosh generated
The following illustrations appear in the children's book "Mr. Lunch Takes a Plane Ride."

When Mr. Lunch woke up, he saw a terrible mess. If anyone else saw this his reputation could be ruined. With little time left he hurried to put things back, but it was hard to remember what went where.

As the captain prepared for landing, Mr. Lunch forgot all about the bags. He realized that he would soon be on television.

...and out to the airport.

The audience was stunned. They sat in silence until the smoke cleared. And then they saw it: a scientific supercake! The chef screamed, "MY MASTERPIECE!"

Richard McGuire

Editor) Howard **Reeves** Date) 1992 Publisher**) Rizzoll International P**ublications, Inc. Medium) **Gou**ache and pencil
This series **of illustrations was created for the "Orange Book,"** which told the story of **fourtee**n oranges
after they had **been picked and had gone their separate ways. This** one's entitled "Six was used **f**or marmalade."

"Nine **was used in a strange experi**ment."

"Eight rolled overboard."

129

"...and **maybe the next one you** eat."

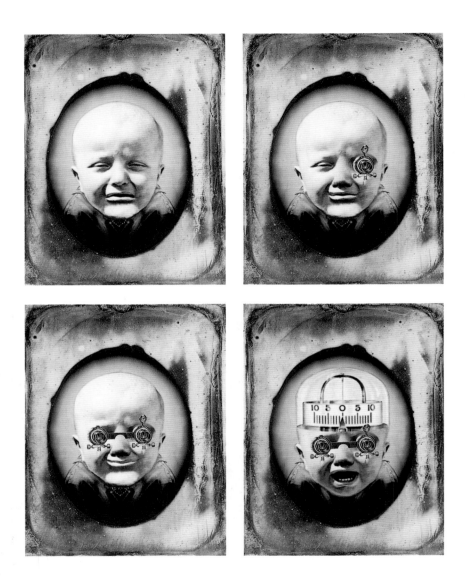

John **Borru**so

Art Director) Bart Nagel Editor) Rudy **Rucker and Queen Mu** **Writer)** R.U. Sirius Book Title) Mondo 2000
A User's Guide **to the New Edge** Date) **November 1992** **Publisher)** **Harper** Collins Publishers, Inc. Medium) Collage
Originally titled "Transformer," this **illustration introduces the** chapter "Evolutionary Mutations."

Date) **December 1992** **Publisher) Brad Burkhart** Publishing Medium) Oil
This illustration appeared in the "Recording Industry Sourcebook."

Mark **Ryd**en

John Collier

Art Director) Alex Jay Editor) Gillian Bucky Writer) Vivian Werner Date) 1992 Publisher) Byron Preiss Visual Publications Medium) Pastel
This series was used as the cover and inside illustrations for the book "Petrouchka - The Story of the Ballet."

"Ballerina on Moor's Lap."

133

"The Magician."

"Petrouchka and the Magician's Flute."

Lilla **Ro**gers

Art Director) **Tomoko Kochi Date) February 1993 Publisher) Fukutake** Publishing Co., Ltd. Medium) Mixed media
This series **of illustrations accompanied the story "The Rainbow M**agicians," **written for a children**'s book.

むらさき

むらさき

Editor) Gary Groth   Date) March 1992   Publisher) Fantagraphics   Medium) Stencil, enamel paint and colored pencils
In response to the Rodney King beating, this illustration appeared on the cover of the comic book "Bleeding Heart #2."

Peter Kuper

141

Art Director) Paul Elliot Writer) D.J. MacHale Date) Winter 1992 Publisher) Rabbit Ears Medium) Pastel
This image of two heads kissing appears in the children's book "East of the Sun, West of the Moon."

Vivienne Flesher

143

Thomas Woodruff

Art Director) Michaela Sullivan Editor) Richard Todd Author) Ann Patchett Date) 1992 Publisher) Houghton Mifflin Company
Medium) Acrylic on linen This illustration appears as the cover for "The Patron Saint of Liars."

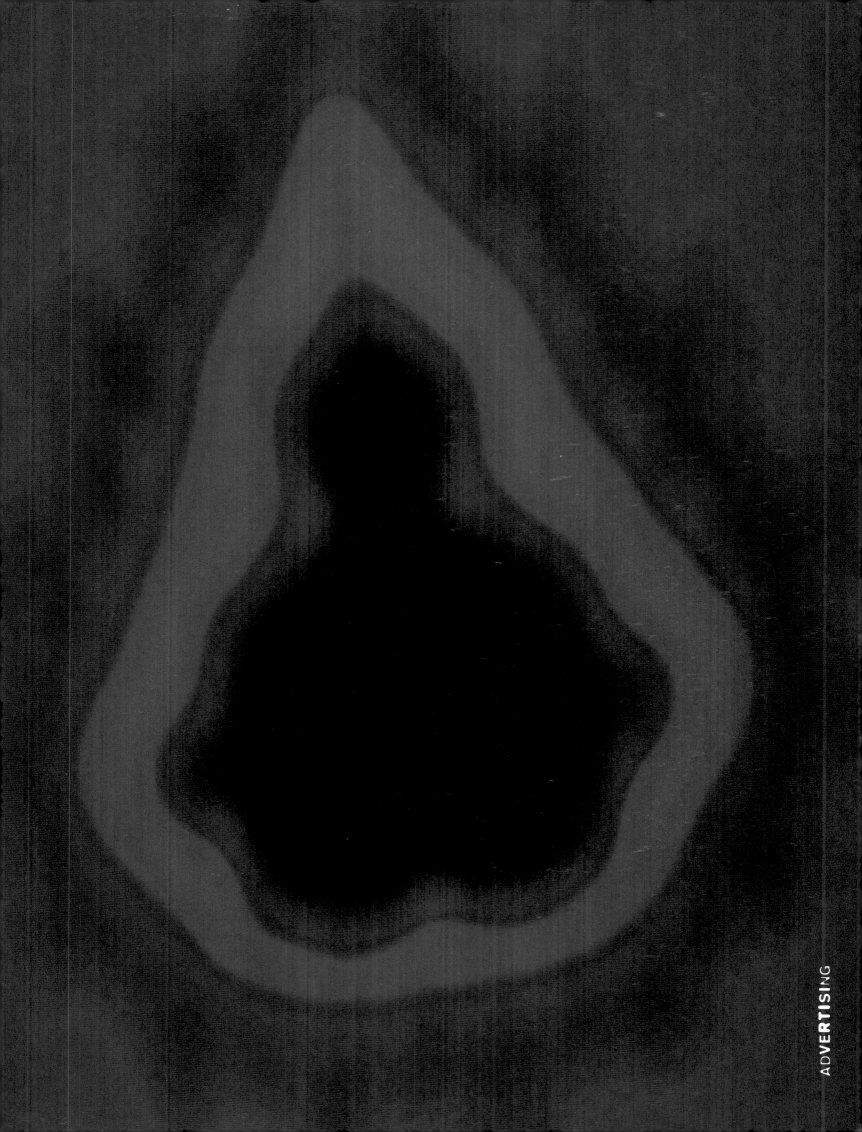

Josh **Gos**field

Art Directors) **Simon Doonan, Tony Kushner and Josh Gosfield   Client)** Barneys New York   **Medium)** Mixed media
This collection of window displays was **created for Barneys New York,** in celebration of Fathers Day, 1992.

Ruth Marten

Art **Director)** Robin Schiff **Publisher) Random House** Medium) Egg tempera on wood
This illustration appeared **in the Random House** Autumn Catalogue, **1992** (above).

∞

Art Director) **Melanie Nissen** Publication) **The Seventh Annual Soul** Train Music Awards **Date)** March 9, 1993
Client) Atlantic Recording **Corporation** Medium) **Collage This collage appea**red in the award show's souvenir program book (left).

Edmund Guy

150

Chesley McLaren

Client) Prix Fixe **Restaurant Medium)** Acrylic on canvas
One in a series of murals entitled "Club de Jazz," created for a New York restaurant.

Art Director) Scott Wadler Designer) Laurie Hinzman and Jennifer Juliano
Client) Comedy Central Medium) Ink This illustration appeared on promotional t-shirts.

Scott Menchin

151

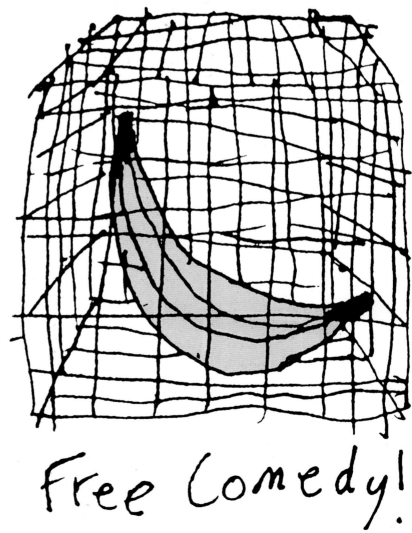

152

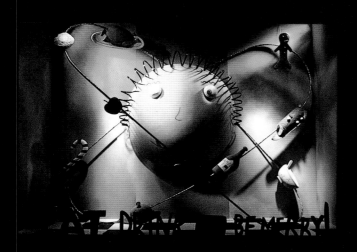

Jessie Hartland

Art Director) Robin M. Lauritano   Client) Bloomingdale's   Medium) Mixed media
This collection of window displays, celebrating **Christmas at Bloomingdale's,** featured objects that moved, spun and nodded.

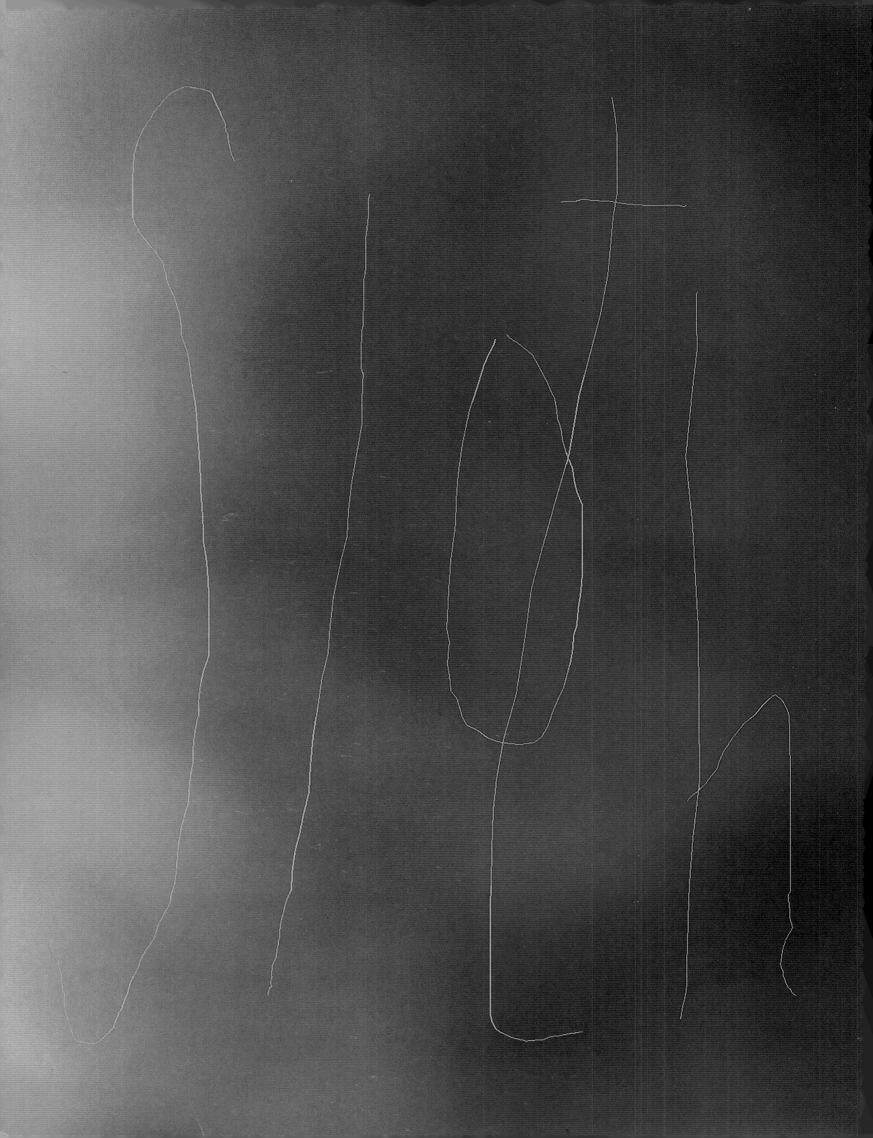

POSTERS/MAPS

Medium) **Ink and chalk on vellum This poster was used as a** promotional piece for HBO/TVKO.

Jill **Buch**anan

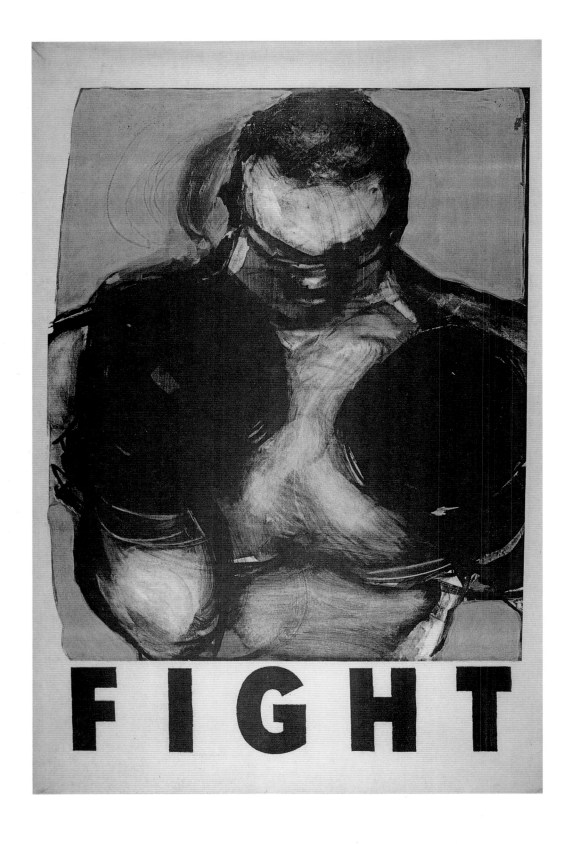

157

Greg Clarke

Medium) Limited edition silkscreen print on rag paper.
This poster was created for an exhibition called "Wisegeist" at the Clay Doyle Gallery in Los Angeles.

158

Art **Garc**ia

Art Directors) Ron Sullivan **and Art Garcia Writers) M**ark Perkins and Priscilla Siegel
Printer) **Williamson Medium) Xerox collage and offset printing This poster was designed to** announce
the **guest speaker, Art Chantry, at a Dallas Society of V**isual Communications **meeti**ng.

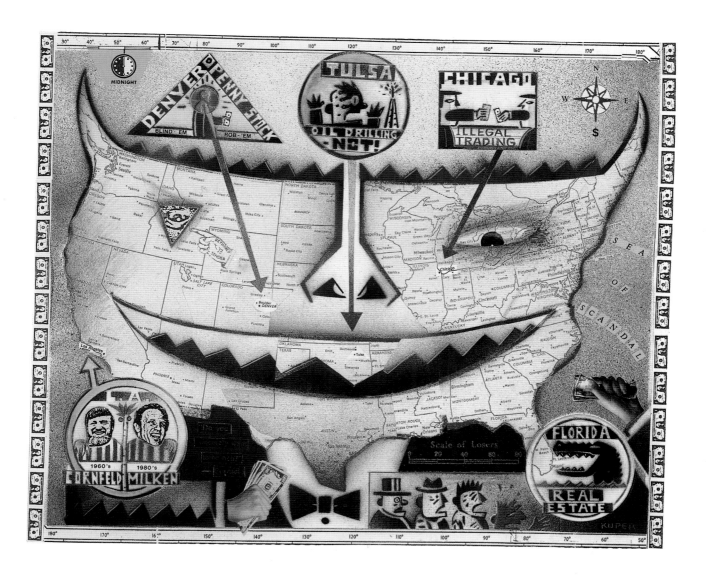

159

Peter **Ku**per

Art **Director)** Kelly McMurray **Writer) John Strahinich Publi**cation) Worth Date) March 1993
Publisher) **Capital Publishing Medium) Mixed media Appearing with** the article "Scams USA," this map is
a guide to various **American investment swindles**, rip-offs and scams.

Lilla ROgers

Art Directors) **Chris Farley and Gina Russell Design Firm) Chermaye**ff and Geismar Medium) **Ink** and cut paper
These **two illustrations appeared as a display for The Woman**'s Rights Museum, Seneca Falls, NY.

FAct: In 1989, 2% of → the executives at Fortune 500 companies were female.

Art Director) Hitoshi Himagawa Agency) Close **World Collection Client**) Sugar for Strawberry **Field**s and Bow Brand
Date) Spring **1993** Medium) **Brush and ink and color tints A prom**otional piece for a **spring cl**othing line.

Isabelle Dervaux

Client) Architects, Designers & Planners for **Social Responsibility Med**ium) Ball point pen on **corru**gated cardboard
This illustration, entitled "**Shelter ca 1990,**" **is curren**tly being sold as a postcard.

Kiyo**shi K**an**ai**

Brian Cronin

Medium) Pen and ink **and letter press printing** A self-promotional piece.

John Craig

Art Director) Gordon Mortensen Design Firm) Mortensen Design Publication) Harnessing Information
Date) Spring 1992 Client) Stanford University, Center for the Study of Languages and Information
Medium) Collage, ink and scratching An informational booklet on robotics and language included this illustration.

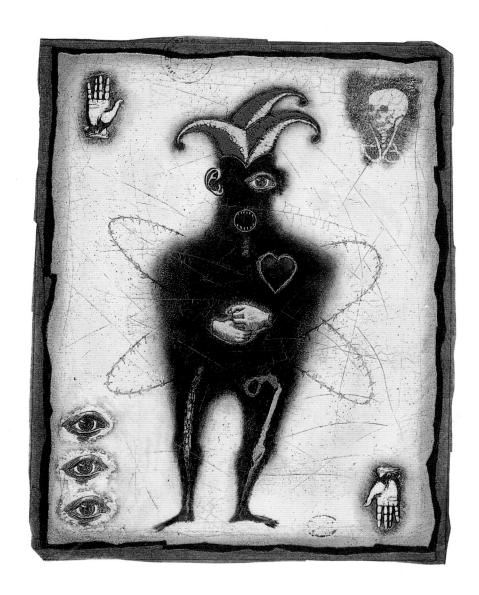

Pol **Turgeo**n

Art **Di**re**ctor)** Lori Siebert   Design **Firm) Siebert Design Ass**ociates, Inc.   **Client)** Beckett Paper
Agency) Northlick, Stolley, La Warre   Writer) Bob **Gard   Date) Winter 1992   Medium)** Photocopy, oil, ink, go**u**ache, tape and varnish
This illustration, part of a promotional series **exploring different emo**tions, represents the emotion hate (above).

∞

Art Dire**ctor)** Sunil Bhandari   Design **Firm) Harris-Bhandari   Writer)** Helen Battersby   **Medium)** Acrylic
With each **suit representing a different season, these playing cards** were sent out as Christmas greetings (left).

Sandra **Dion**isi

Bill **Ma**yer

Art Director) Jerry Sullivan Client) Graphic Ads Medium) Gouache and dyes
This ad, entitled "Graphic Ads is **Having an Identity Crisis,"** ran originally in Ego **Magazine** (below).

∞

Art Director) Kim Champagne **Client) Warner Brothers Records Date) August 11, 1992 Medium) Multi-media** three dimensional art
This illustration was created for **the Elmore James "King of** the Slide Guitar" CD package (right).

Josh **Gos**field

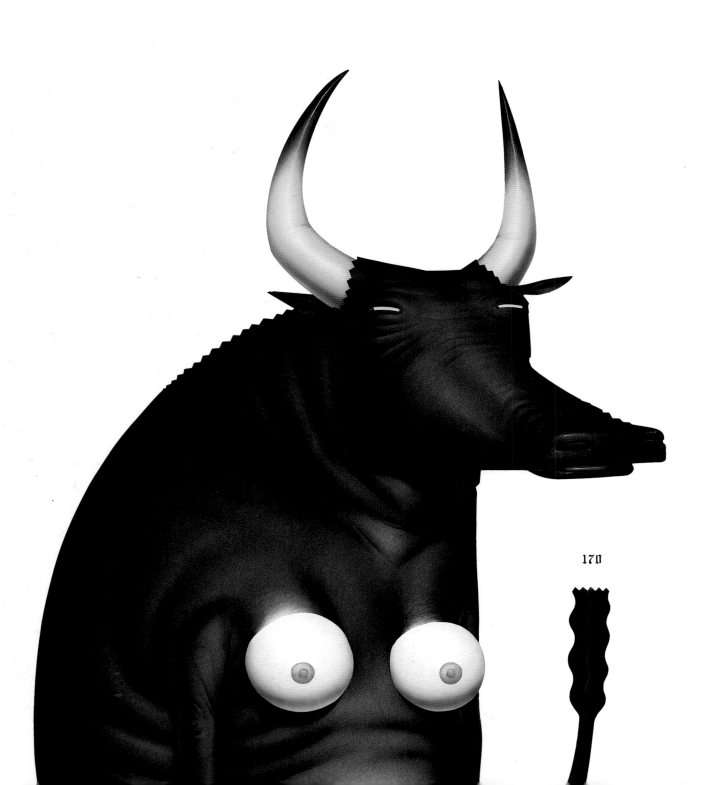

170

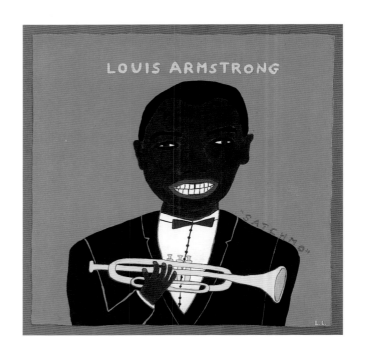

Laura Levine

172

Art Director) Alli Truch   Client) **Verve/Polygram Records**   Medium) Acrylic on masonite
These portraits appeared on the CD covers of the "Essential Series."

173

Christian Northeast

Medium) Mixed media The following three images were created for the illustrator's portfolio.

177

Medium) Acrylics, spray paint and cardboard A personal work entitled "Firewater."

Gerald **Busta**mante

179

∞

Ruth Marten

Medium) Egg **tempera on wood** **"Havana** Red" (above).

∞

Medium) Egg **tempera on wood** **"Portralt** of Saul" (right).

Medium) Acrylic   A personal piece entitled "Being Fat in the USA."

Lisa Manning

BEING **F A T** IN THE **U S A**

182

Marie Lessard

Medium) Linocut and **transfer on paper** **An un**titled personal work.

Tim Lewis

Medium) **Water color over Xeroxed copy of drawing** **A personal** piece entitled "Plate Spinner" (above).

∞

Medium) **Water color over Xeroxed copy** of drawing
Entitled "Profile Puzzle," the **figures are holding shapes** that form another profile (right).

Beth **O'Gra**dy

Medium) Pen and ink, gouache **A self-promotional piec**e completed in June 1992.

Irene Rofheart Pigott

Medium) Oil on **paper** **This illustration was created for self-promotio**nal purposes, entitled "**Portrai**t of a Woman."

Art Director) Jim Christie **Client)** Bloomingdale's **Medium)** Acrylic paints on paper
For the new store campaign, "Only at Bloomingdale's," this shopping bag was commissioned, but never used.

Jessie Hartland

Richard Downs

Medium) Mixed media This is the **artist's interpretation** of "Life and Love in the Big City."

Laura Levine

Medium) Acrylic on masonite with antique frame
This portrait of B.B. King is one in a series of musicians for a show at the Julie Rico Gallery.

Terry Allen

Medium) Gouache A personal piece entitled "Cool," May 1992.

Andrew Powell

Medium) **Acrylic, collage and pastel** **This illustration explores** the image of the long-lost cowboy.

Medium) Oil and **acrylic** **A personal work** about smoking.

Calef Brown

Medium) **Oil and acrylic This illustration was created for a pro**posed children's book about death.

Calef Brown

195

D.P
The future is not some place we are going to, but one we are
Creating. The paths to it are made, not found and the activity
of making them changes both the maker and the destination

Darren Pryce

This personal piece, entitled "Agency **2003**," depicts the world after its complete ozone depletion.

Amy Guip

Medium) **Collage Untitled perso**nal work.

Medium) Alkyd on paper A personal piece entitled "Spaz the Cat."

Greg Clarke

Art Director) Michael Walsh Medium) Ink and watercolor This commissioned but unpublished book jacket is in part a self-portrait. The illustrator wore a rubber gorilla nose during the execution.

Alan E. Cober

Philippe Lardy

Art Director) Alison Grevstad Client) Nordstrom Publication) Employee Benefits / Program Cover Medium) Gouache
A different version of this illustration will appear in an upcoming brochure describing Nordstrom's employee benefits.

VIDEO

ADVARTICE

Brad **Holl**and

Creative Director) Parry Merkley Art Director) **Guy Marino** Copywriter) Bill Stone Agency) Merkley Newman Harty
Client) Bankers Trust Company This video for Bankers Trust Company entitled "Fish/Island" began running in October 1992 on CNN.

Geoffrey Grahn

Animators) Rob Palmer, Kate Flather and Geoffrey Grahn Art Director) Kate Flather Writer) Mark Fenske
Agency) Creative Artists Agency Production Company) The Bomb Factory Client) Coca-Cola Sound) Warren Dewey Medium) Scratchboard,
Macintosh computer with Adobe Photoshop and Macromind Director "Coca-Cola Time Line," a thirty-second
animated televison commercial, began airing nationally in February 1993 and internationally in March 1993.

Mark Marek

Animator) Mike De Seve Art Director) R.O. Blechman Production Company) The Ink Tank
This sequence, from a promotional thirty-five second reel opener, was created in-house for the Ink Tank.

Index

Terry Allen
164 Daniel Low Terrace
Staten Island, NY 10301
61/191

Michael Bartalos
4222 18th Street
San Francisco, CA 94114
106

Gary Baseman
443 12th Street #2D
Brooklyn, NY 11215
37

Benoît
c/o Riley Illustration
155 West 15th Street #4C
New York, NY 10011
73

Maris Bishofs
251-16 Northern Boulevard
Little Neck, NY 11363
57

Patrick Blackwell
P.O. Box 324, Pond Road
North Truro, MA 02652
86

Barry Blitt
34 Lincoln Avenue
Greenwich, CT 06830
16/102

John Borruso
1259 Guerrero Street
San Francisco, CA 94110
130

Steve Brodner
120 Cabrini Boulevard
New York, NY 10033
40-41

Calef Brown
15339 Camarillo Street
Sherman Oaks, CA 91403
97/193/194

Jill Buchanan
168 Ludlow Street
New York, NY 10002
156

Charles Burns
210 Brown Street
Philadelphia, PA 19123
33-36

Gerald Bustamante
4528 North 44th Street
San Diego, CA 92115
179

Stephen Byram
52 68th Street #1
Guttenberg, NJ 07093
29

Greg Clarke
844 Ninth Street #10
Santa Monica, CA 90403
157/197

Christian Clayton
10730 E. Bethany Drive, Suite 204
Aurora, CO 80014
89

Alan E. Cober
95 Croton Dam Road
Ossining, NY 10562
198

Sue Coe
214 East 84th Street #3C
New York, NY 10028
31/32

John Collier
c/o Richard Solomon
121 Madison Avenue #5F
New York, NY 10016
132-135

John Craig
Tower Road Route 2, Box 2224
Soldiers Grove, WI 54655
167

Brian Cronin
"Montmolin" Royal Terrace Lane
Dun Laoghaire, Co Dublin, Ireland
58/75/166

Georganne Deen
3834 Aloha Street
Los Angeles, CA 90027
24

Isabelle Dervaux
c/o Riley Illustration
155 West 15th Street #4C
New York, NY 10011
164

David Diaz
6708 Corintia Street
Rancho La Costa, CA 92009
114-117

Eric Dinyer
5510 Holmes
Kansas City, MO 64110
78

Sandra Dionisi
128 MacDonell Avenue
Toronto, Ontario
Canada M6R 2A5
98/168

Richard Downs
24294 Saradella Court
Murrieta, CA 92562
80/189

Blair Drawson
14 Leuty Avenue
Toronto, Ontario
Canada M4E 2R3
20/44

Henrik Drescher
c/o Reactor Art & Design
51 Camden Street
Toronto, Ontario
Canada M5V 1V2
82

Jeffrey Fisher
c/o Riley Illustration
155 West 15th Street #4C
New York, NY 10011
59/87

Vivienne Flesher
194 3rd Avenue
New York, NY 10003
142

Art Garcia
c/o Richelle Munn
2811 McKinney Avenue
Suite 320, LB111
Dallas, TX 75204
158

Josh Gosfield
682 Broadway #4A
New York, NY 10012
53/146-147/171

Geoffrey Grahn
9927 Braddock Drive
Culver City, CA 90232
202-203

Steven Guarnaccia
430 West 14th Street #508
New York, NY 10014
107/108

Amy Guip
352 Bowery #2
New York, NY 10012
67-69/196

Edmund Guy
820 Hudson Street
Hoboken, NJ 07030
27/148

Jessie Hartland
165 William Street
New York, NY 10038
152-153/188

Sandra Hendler
1823 Spruce Street
Philadelphia, PA 19103
23

Brad Holland
96 Greene Street
New York, NY 10012
26/76/85/92/201

Jason Holley
664 Monterey Rd.
So. Pasadena, CA 91030
83

David Hughes
43 Station Road
Marple Cheshire,
England SV66AJ
38

Jordin Isip
44 4th Place #2
Brooklyn, NY 11231
46-48

Frances Jetter
390 West End Avenue
New York, NY 10024
43/111

Joel Peter Johnson
P.O. Box 803 Ellicott Station
Buffalo, NY 14205-0803
84

Maira Kalman
59 West 12th Street
New York, NY 10011
19

Kiyoshi Kanai
115 East 30th Street
New York, NY 10016
165

Brian Krueger
P.O. Box 6290
Cincinnati, OH 45206
66

Peter Kuper
250 West 99th Street #9C
New York, NY 10025
141/159

Philippe Lardy
478 West Broadway #5A
New York, NY 10012
101/199

Marie Lessard
4641 Hutchison
Montreal, Quebec
Canada H2V 4A2
183

Laura Levine
444 Broome Street
New York, NY 10013
172-173/190

Tim Lewis
184 St. Johns Place
Brooklyn, NY 11217-3402
184/185

Warren Linn
4915 Broadway #2A
New York, NY 10034
28/96

Matt Mahurin
666 Greenwich Street #16
New York, NY 10014
79

Lisa Manning
12 Ledge Lane
Gloucester, MA 01930
182

Mark Marek
199 Owatonna Street
Haworth, NJ 07641
202-203

Ruth Marten
8 West 13th Street #7RW
New York, NY 10011
149/180-181

Bill Mayer
240 Forkner Drive
Decatur, GA 30030
170

Richard McGuire
45 Carmine Street #3B
New York, NY 10014
126-129

Chesley McLaren
228 West 82nd Street
New York, NY 10024
150

Scott Menchin
640 Broadway
New York, NY 10012
109/110/151

Christian Northeast
48 Abell Street #245
Toronto, Ontario
Canada M6J 3H2
54-56/176-178

José Ortega
524 East 82nd Street
New York, NY 10028
81/100

Beth O'Grady
161 Fourth Street #3E
Hoboken, NJ 07030
186

C.F. Payne
758 Springfield Pike
Cincinnati, OH 45215
94/95

Hanoch Piven
310 West 22nd Street #4A
New York, NY 10011
62-65

David Plunkert
3647 Falls Road
Baltimore, MD 21211
49-52/72/74

Andrew Powell
420 North 5th Street #706
Minneapolis, MN 55401
192

Darren Pryce
90 Clyde Street St. Kilda
Victoria 3182 Australia
195

Robert Risko
155 West 15th Street #4B
New York, NY 10011
39

Irene Rofheart Pigott
75 Prospect Park West #1A
Brooklyn, NY 11215-3054
187

Lilla Rogers
6 Parker Road
Arlington, MA 02178
136-140/162-163

Jonathon Rosen
408 Second Street #3
Brooklyn, NY 11215
90-91/104-105

Mark Ryden
221 West Maple
Monrovia, CA 91016
131

Wiktor Sadowski
c/o Marlena Torzecka
211 East 89th Street, Suite A-1
New York, NY 10128
45

Rick Sealock
112 C 17th Avenue N.W.
Calgary, Alberta
Canada T2M 0M6
88

J. Otto Seibold
38 West 21st Street 11th Floor
New York, NY 10010
122-125

Lane Smith
12 West 18th Street #6W
New York, NY 10011
118-121

Owen Smith
4370 Faulkner Drive
Fremont, CA 94536
30

Edward Sorel
156 Franklin Street
New York, NY 10013
22

Ralph Steadman
c/o Andrea Harding
146 East 19th Street
New York, NY 10003
42

Gary Tanhauser
3018 Orange Avenue
Santa Ana, CA 92707
70-71

Malcolm Tarlofsky
P.O. Box 786
Glen Ellen, CA 95442
77

Pol Turgeon
5187 Jeanne-Mance #3
Montreal, Quebec
Canada H2V 4K2
169

Maurice Vellekoop
c/o Reactor Art & Design
51 Camden Street
Toronto, Ontario
Canada M5V 1V2
21

Stefano Vitale
478 Bergen Street #4
Brooklyn, NY 11217
99

Alexandra Weems
58 East 80th Street #2B
New York, NY 10021
17/18

Philippe Weisbecker
c/o Riley Illustration
155 West 15th Street #4C
New York, NY 10011
103

Mick Wiggins
1103 Amador Avenue
Berkeley, CA 94707
60

Thomas Woodruff
29 Cornelia Street #17
New York, NY 10014
143

Janet Woolley
c/o Alan Lynch
11 Kings Ridge Road
Long Valley, NJ 07853
25/93

Art/Creative Directors and Designers

Anderson, Gail 63, 80
Armario, David 61, 104-105
Baker, Richard 38, 109
Bartholomay, Lucy 75, 86
Berry, Pamela 19, 20, 41, 56
Betts, Elizabeth 64
Bhandari, Sunil 168
Birch, Linda 106
Black, Roger 73
Blechman, R.O. 202-203
Carson, David
    47, 67-69, 78, 89, 91
Caruso, Leigh 50-52
Champagne, Kim 171
Christie, Jim 188
Chu, Michele 57
Churchward, Charles 39
Colyer, Martin 58
Cook, Tim 98, 99
Curry, Chris 16-18, 34, 62
Dazzo, Susan Gockel 37
Diaz, Cecelia 114-118
Diaz, David 114-118
Dizney, Joseph 59
Doe, Kelly 38, 109
Doonan, Simon 146-147
Duckworth, Nancy 97
Elliot, Paul 142
Evans, Mark 49
Farley, Chris 162-163
Ferrand, Jaime 96
Ferrell, Joan 45
Fillebrown, Tom 83
Flather, Kate 202-203
Flinchum, Dwayne 23, 84
Frank, Laura N. 48, 54-55
Frey, Jane 25
Froelich, Janet 30
Garcia, Art 158
Garlan, Judy 24
Gilman, Jennifer 111
Gosfield, Josh 146-147
Grevstad, Alison 199
Grossman, Michael 64
Helfand, Jessica 100
Himagawa, Hitoshi 164
Hinzman, Laurie 151
Hoffman, Cindy 107
Hoffman, Joanne 60

Hoglund, Rudolph C. 25
Honeycutt, B.W. 90
Ilić, Mirko 28, 29
Innes, Claire 88
Jay, Alex 132-135
Juliano, Jennifer 151
Kochi, Tomoko 136-140
Koudys, Mark 102
Kushner, Tony 146-147
Lambertus, James 104
Latis, Silvia 108
Lauritano, Robin M. 152-153
Leach, Molly 118-121
Littrell, Kandy 30
Loewy, David 74
Lorenz, Lee 16
Maddocks, Victoria 96
Marino, Guy 201
McMurray, Kelly 159
Merkley, Parry 201
Mitchell, Pat 70
Mortensen, Gordon 167
Nagel, Bart 130
Nissen, Melanie 148
Palecek, Jane 44, 53, 71, 79
Perry, Darrin 21
Pope, Kerig 26
Powers, Lisa 43
Priest, Robert 36, 94, 95
Routhier, Chuck 77
Rubinstein, Rhonda 87
Russell, Gina 162-163
Ruys, Suzette 23, 84
Sanford, John 76
Schiff, Robin 149
Siebert, Lori 169
Skelton, Claude 72
Sloane, Chris 103
Smith, Adam 40
Staebler, Tom 26
Stearns, Sarah 101
Sullivan, Jerry 170
Sullivan, Michaela 143
Sullivan, Ron 158
Suzuki, Tom 98, 99
Thompson, Kate 46, 110
Tremain, Kerry 85
Truch, Alli 172
Wadler, Scott 151
Walsh, Michael 198
Woodward, Fred 22, 27, 31, 32,
    33, 35, 42, 63, 66, 80, 82, 92-93

Animators

De Seve, Mike 202-203
Flather, Kate 202-203
Grahn, Geoffrey 202-203
Palmer, Rob 202-203

Editors

Auchincloss, Kenneth 43
Arthaud, Katherine 96
Beatty, Jack 24
Brown, Tina 16-18, 34, 62
Bucky, Gillian 132-135
Duffy, Jim 49
Emmrich, Stuart 59
Ewing-Pearse, Betty 102
Foell, Earl W. 48, 54-55
Gadsby, Patricia 104-105
Gergen, David 57
Groth, Gary 141
Guccione, Bob 23, 84
Hayes, Regina 118-121
Hoffman, Paul 104-105
Hunt, Chris 21
Inman, William 101
Israel, Bret 97
Jarrett, Marvin Scott
    47, 67-69, 78, 89, 91
Jimenez, Sandy 81
Jones, Sabrina 81
Lazar, Florence 74
Mark, M. 46
McDonell, Terry 73, 87
McGeary, Johanna 25
Minetto, Renato 108
Mu, Queen 130
O'Donnell, Bob 106
Ravgiala, Gail 107
Reeves, Howard 126-129
Rice, Jim 72
Rome, Avery 100
Ruby, Daniel 77
Rucker, Rudy 130
Schrier, Eric 44, 53, 71, 79
Shipley, David 28, 29
Sylvain, Rick 88
Thompson, Bob 38, 109
Tobocman, Seth 81
Todd, Richard 143
Weidenbaum, Marc 83
Weinman, Steve 58
Wilburn, Deborah 45
Zellman, Ande 75, 86

Writers

Agnelli, Lauren 67
Alden, Grant 66
Allen, Dave 68-69
Anderson, Steve 57
Andreopoulos, Spyros 61
Atkinson, Mark A. 98
Battersby, Helen 168
Beck, Melinda 88
Bergson, Eliot 77
Breen, Bill 70
Brisbin, Shelly 60
Brzezinski, Zbigniew 48
Buford, Bill 30
Carlson, Peter 38
Clute, Kathleen 37
Cohen, Susan 109
Coleman, Mark 27
Davis, Erik 46
Devitt, Jon 58
Diamant, Anita 75
Dolnick, Edward 53, 79
Dovidio, John 52
Fenske, Mark 202-203
Friedman, Steve 36
Galagan, Patricia A. 50/51
Gard, Bob 169
Gates Jr., Henry Louis 110
Gibilisco, Stan 96
Gibney Jr., Frank 43
Gitter, Mike 83
Graves, Keith 58
Haley, Alex 26
Harrison, Jim 73
Heilbroner, Robert 72
Ho, Elizabeth 111
Isler, Scott 80
Kaminer, Wendy 24
Kaplan, Michael 19
Keane, Fergal 58
Kohan, John 25
Laidlaw, Marc 84
Lowenstein, Jerold M. 104-105
Lyons, James 59
MacHale, D.J. 142
Markusen, Ann 28
Maas, Peter 87
McGill, Douglas C. 101

McKillop, Peter 43

Moreau, Dan 103

Mortimer, John 95

Oppenheimer, Larry 106

Ortega, José 81

Patchett, Ann 143

Perkins, Mark 158

Powell, Bill 43

Reed, Kit 23

Ressner, Jeffrey 56

Rodriguez, Louis J. 100

Rosack, T. 29

Scanlon, Charles 58

Schneider, Stephen H. 54-55

Schover, Leslie 99

Scieszka, Jon 118-121

Seibold, J. Otto 122-125

Sharp, David 44

Siegel, Paula 45

Siegel, Priscilla 158

Sirius, R.U. 130

Smith, Gary 21

Steinbaum, Ellen 107

Stilgoe, John R. 86

Stone, Bill 201

Strahinich, John 159

Strasser, Steven 43

Summers, Anthony 39

Thompson, Hunter S. 42

Travers, Peter 22, 32, 63

Tucker, Ken 64

Vidal, Gore 94

Vienne, Veronique 85

Wach, Bonnie 71

Walsh, Vivian 122-125

Waugh, Eric 58

Wehrfritz, George 43

Werner, Vivian 132-135

Whitehead, Kevin 49

Wilkinson, Scott 106

Winter, William E. 98

Wright, Lawrence 82

Publications

Abitare 108

American Health Magazine 37

The Atlantic Monthly 24

Bleeding Heart #2 141

Bloomberg Magazine 101

The Boston Globe 107

The Boston Globe Magazine 75, 86

BBC Worldwide 58

City Paper 49

Details 90

Detroit Free Press 88

Diabetes Forecast 98-99

Digital News 102

Discover Magazine 104-105

East of the Sun, West of the Moon 142

Electronic Musician 106

Entertainment Weekly 64

Esquire 87

Esquire Sportsman 73

Garbage Magazine 70

GQ Magazine 36, 94, 95

Harnessing Information 167

Health 44, 53, 71, 79

Kiplinger's Personal Finance Magazine 103

The Los Angeles Times Magazine 97

Macworld 39

Mirabella 40

Mondo 2000 130

Mother Jones 85

Mr. Lunch Takes a Plane Ride 122-125

The New York Times 28, 29

The New York Times Magazine 30

The New Yorker 16-18, 34, 62

Newsweek International 43

NeXTWORLD 77

Omni Magazine 23, 84

The Orange Book 126-129

The Patron Saint of Liars 143

Petrouchka–The Story of the Ballet 132-135

Philadelphia Inquirer Magazine 100

Playboy 26

Pulse! 83

Random House Autumn Catalogue 149

Ray Gun 47, 67-69, 78, 89, 91

Recording Industry Sourcebook 131

Rolling Stone 22, 27, 31-33, 35, 42, 63, 66, 80, 82, 92-93

Russia Special Issue of Time Magazine 25

The Seventh Annual Soul Train Music Awards Program 148

Smart Money 59

South Beach Magazine 96

Sports Illustrated 21

Stanford Medicine 61

The Stinky Cheese Man and other Fairly Stupid Tales 118-121

Sweet Peas 114-118

TLC Monthly 76

Training and Development Magazine 50-52

US Magazine 19, 20, 41, 56

U.S. News and World Report 57

Vanity Fair 39

Varbusiness 74

The Village Voice 110, 111

Voice Literary Supplement 46

Washington Monthly 72

The Washington Post Magazine 38, 109

Working Mother Magazine 45

World Monitor Magazine 48, 54-55

World War Three 81

Worth 159

Publishing Companies

Abitare Segesta 108

Act III Publishing 106

Affiliated Publications, Inc. 75, 86, 107

American Diabetes Association, Inc. 98, 99

American Society for Training and Development 50-52

The Atlantic Monthly Company 24

Brad Burkhart Publishing 131

Byron Preiss Visual Publications 132-135

Capital City Publications 72

Capital Publishing 159

The Christian Science Publishing Society 48, 54-55

CMP Publications 74

Condé Nast Publications, Inc. 16-18, 34, 36, 39, 62, 90, 94, 95

Digital Equipment of Canada, Ltd. 102

Discovery Communications 76

Disney Magazine Publishing, Inc. 104-105

Dovetale Publishers 70

Fantagraphics 141

Foundation for National Progress 85

Fukutake Publishing Co., Ltd. 136-140

General Media Publication Group 23, 84

Harper Collins Publishers, Inc. 130

Houghton Mifflin Company 143

The Hearst Corporation 73, 87

Hearst & Dow Jones 59

Hippocrates Partners 44, 53, 71, 79

Icon Books 114-117

Integrated Media 77

Kiplinger Washington Editors 103

Knight-Ridder 88, 100

Lang Communications 45

Macworld Communications, Inc. 60

Michael Bloomberg Publishing 101

MTS Inc. 83

Murdoch Publications 40

New York Times Company
28, 29, 30

Playboy Enterprises, Inc. 26

Rabbit Ears 142

Random House 149

Ray Gun Publishing, Inc.
47, 67, 68-69, 78, 89, 91

Reader's Digest
Publications, Inc. 37

Rizzoli International
Publications, Inc. 126-129

Scranton Times 49

South Beach Magazine, Inc. 96

Stanford University 61

Straight Arrow Publishers, Inc.
19, 20, 22, 27, 31-33, 35, 41,
42, 56, 63, 66, 80, 82, 92, 93

The Time Inc. Magazine
Company 21, 25, 64

Times Mirror 97

Viking Books 118-125

VV Publishing Corporation
46, 110, 111

The Washington Post Company
38, 43, 109

World Color Press 57

Advertising Agencies

Close World Collection 164

Creative Artists Agency 202-203

Merkley Newman Harty 201

Northlick, Stolley, La Warre 169

Clients

Architects, Designers & Planners
for Social Responsibility 165

Atlantic Recording Corporation 148

Bankers Trust Company 201

Barneys New York 146-147

Beckett Paper 169

Bloomingdale's 152-153, 188

Coca-Cola 202-203

Comedy Central 151

Dallas Society of Visual
Communications 158

Graphic Ads 170

HBO/TVKO 156

Nordstrom 199

Prix Fixe Restaurant 150

Stanford University 167

Sugar for Strawberry Fields and
Bow Brand 164

Verve/Polygram Records 172

Warner Brothers Records 171

Design Firms

Chermayeff and Giesmar 162-163

Harris-Bhandari 168

Mortensen Design 167

Siebert Design Associates, Inc. 169

Studio J 132-135

Tom Suzuki Design, Inc. 98, 99

Production/Studios

The Bomb Factory 202-203

The Ink Tank 202-203

Sound

Warren Dewey 202-203